ELEPHANTS
THE VANISHING GIANTS

Dan Freeman

ELEPHANTS
THE VANISHING GIANTS

Dan Freeman

G.P. Putnam's Sons, New York

A BISON BOOK

CONTENTS

Introduction

The elephant is now a threatened species. As most people will agree, this is tragic. It is not enough to lament the elephants' fate, admire their charm and power, and accuse ourselves of pushing them toward extinction. True, gross exploitation and barbarity have contributed to their decline, but there are complex social and ecological questions involved which demand close analysis. Take, as a starting point, the evolutionary decline of the elephants and their relatives – the wider framework within which the question of conservation must be seen.

For the truth is that when *Homo sapiens*, 'thinking man,' arrived as a new mark on the tree of evolution a million or more years ago, the order to which elephants belong was already the decaying stump of a once sturdy branch.

The Proboscidea, 'animals with trunks,' were formerly represented by an array of species which covered much of the world. Today the order is sparsely represented by the rabbit-like hyraxes, the massive seal-like dugongs, the manatees, and the elephants themselves from Africa and Southeast Asia. That order, which groups in all some 350 species spread over a period of 50 million years, has been declining steadily for over three million years.

Why the order went into such a decline is something of a mystery. Some specialists have suggested that the advent of man was the cause. Although such an idea seems plausible in the light of much of our behavior today, it is questionable that our influence could have been quite so far-reaching all those millions of years ago.

There are many reasons for the decline of a species, only few of which are understood. Consider the disappearance of the dinosaurs 65 million years ago, a mass extinction still only partially explained by climatic changes and the resulting ecological disturbances. Such declines,

however, have been an integral part of the evolutionary process since life began over 3000 million years ago.

This in no way absolves us from our responsibilities toward the elephants. They are mistreated because their interests clash with our own, and they are exploited for financial gain. We are thus pushing the elephant toward a perhaps premature extinction, for short-term reasons. Man could be seen to be distorting the evolutionary process, and possibly hastening the demise of one of the earth's most dramatic and appealing creatures. The world's leading conservationists believe that this decline should be halted. This can only be accomplished within the context of an understanding of the creatures' needs. Understanding and conservation: these are the two themes that run through my own interest in elephants, and which underlie the writing of this book.

1: ELEPHANT ORIGINS

Previous page: A scene on Manhattan Island – a mere quarter of a million years ago. An American mastodon sniffs the breeze suspiciously, protective of his herd.

Within our own recorded history elephants have formed an almost continuous series of populations from Africa to China. We have whittled them down to two main groups, African and Asian elephants, which are now separated by several thousand miles. The two groups are not the distant remnants of the same species. Indeed, they are sufficiently different to be classified as separate genera. How and by what means did the elephant arrive at its present-day status and distribution? In tracing their origins there are two lines of investigation. The first is to look at the order Proboscidea, the large complex of families to which they belong, and the second is to isolate the elephant family (the *Elephantidae*) within the order and trace the origins of the two living genera of today.

It is not an easy task because so much fossil evidence must still be buried underground and the conclusions to which every research worker is drawn are inevitably subjective. Thus, as always when the evidence is inconclusive, there is room for argument. Perhaps the simplest way to tackle the subject is to paint the traditional picture of proboscidian evolution and then show how some recent research has deviated from the long-accepted portrait of elephant history within this group.

The great age of the mammals began at the end of the Cretaceous period some 65 million years ago, when the present-day continents were in the process of separating from the single super-continent, Pangaea. It seems most likely that the mammals' evolutionary bloom was triggered by the climatic changes which signalled the downfall of the reptiles, rulers of the earth for nearly 140 million years previously. The earliest proboscidian-like creature to have been found shows many of the features of being a water-dependent animal. This creature was named *Moeritherium* and it came to light at the turn of the twentieth century in the Fayum Depression of Egypt, the northeast corner of Africa that was then a swampy region quite unlike the desert area that it is today. The *Moeritherium* was a small hippopotamus-like, swamp-bound mammal. It possessed neither trunk nor tusks, although both upper and lower jaws housed teeth showing a slight elongation. The closest relatives of *Moeritherium* evolved along separate lines which finally gave rise to the hyraxes and the sea-cow groups of today. So there is some truth in the reasoning that the elephant's closest living relative is the diminutive hyrax. However, the relationship is a distant one: both having gone their separate ways for about 60 million years.

Other finds at the Fayum site in Egypt included *Paleomastodon* and *Phiomia*, both elephant-like in essentials and belonging to the Oligocene period, nearly 20 million years later than *Moeritherium*.

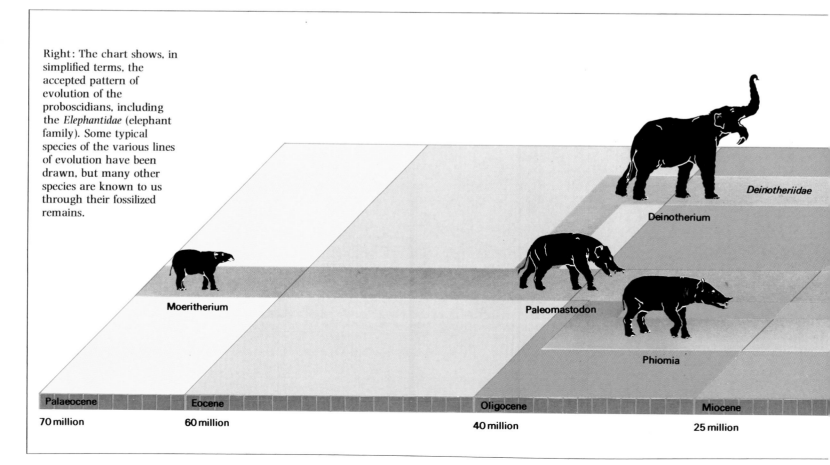

Right: The chart shows, in simplified terms, the accepted pattern of evolution of the proboscidians, including the *Elephantidae* (elephant family). Some typical species of the various lines of evolution have been drawn, but many other species are known to us through their fossilized remains.

Moeritherium

Paleomastodon

Phiomia

Deinotherium

Deinotheriidae

Palaeocene	Eocene	Oligocene	Miocene
70 million	60 million	40 million	25 million

Left: The little African rock hyrax may be considered the nearest living relative to the elephant.

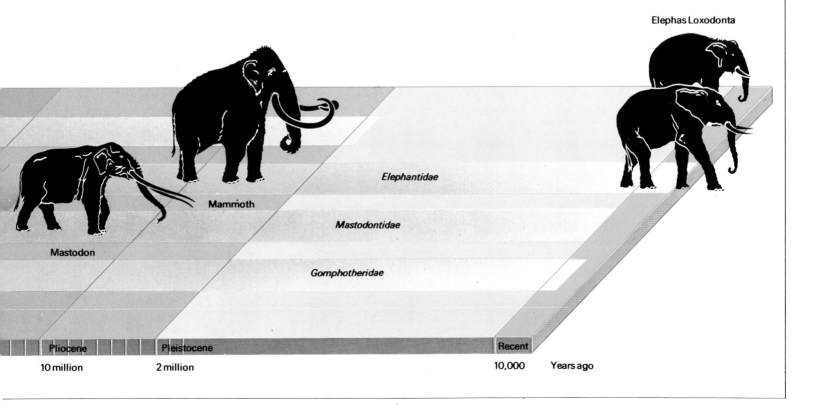

Elephas Loxodonta

Elephantidae

Mastodontidae

Mammoth

Gomphotheridae

Mastodon

Pliocene   Pleistocene   Recent

10 million   2 million   10,000   Years ago

They were large animals and they possessed tusks in both upper and lower jaws. Perhaps their strangest feature was the elongation and strengthening of their lips and jaws to enable them to feed by grasping leaves and grasses. Of the two, *Paleomastodon* shows the closest beginnings of a trunk, which may have enabled it to feed higher off the ground, among the lower branches of trees which it pulled toward its mouth.

It is conceivable that these three animals, *Moeritherium*, *Phiomia*, and *Paleomastodon*, formed part of a basic proboscidian stock from which the true elephant family was one day to evolve. Exactly which of them was responsible is almost impossible to say. Each had begun to assume unique characteristics that were taking them away from each other, both morphologically and ecologically. Their remains have been found only in Africa, so with the available evidence it is reasonable to conclude that the order Proboscidea arose on that continent and then spread out across the world via land-bridges that do not exist today. At that time, America was still close to Europe, and the sea was at times very much lower than its present level. These conditions help to explain the fossil remains of elephant types on the Mediterranean islands of Crete, Malta, and Cyprus. The animals did not swim to these locations; they were isolated on high spots of land when the sea level rose and cut them off from the mainland. This happened sufficiently long ago for new species of dwarf elephants to have evolved on the small islands before they became extinct there.

By the Miocene period, some 35 million years ago, a host of proboscidians had radiated from Africa to Europe, Asia, and North America, all of which were connected. Among them were the deinotheres, a remarkably stable group which existed for more than 40 million years. They were big animals, almost the size of contemporary elephants and although they had large tusks, these came from the lower jaw and turned down sharply so that their points faced almost backward. They may have been used for raking food from the edge and bottom of swamps. The possession of a shortish trunk may have enabled them to breathe above water at the same time. Anyone who has seen a modern elephant completely submerged except for the tip of its trunk could not doubt the river-fording advantages of such an appendage. Any animal that fed on submerged vegetation would reap enormous dividends as well. These ultrasuccessful deinotheres survived until comparatively recently. They did not become extinct until two or three million years ago.

Another formidable group contained the gomphotheres. They also flourished across much of the globe and their weighty, long-tusked influence reached far into the dawn of humanity. Indeed, the better known of them, the long-jawed mastodons, were contemporaries of modern man. The remains of one species of them have been found in caves alongside human artifacts dated as recently as 300 AD. Again, it would be misleading to incriminate humans in the extinction of a group that was a good 10–15 million years past its evolutionary prime.

The true mastodons – a different group from those just mentioned – can be traced along a different evolutionary pathway. Although the two groups showed many superficial similarities, they actually enjoyed a widely separated relationship. *Phiomia* and *Paleomastodon* may represent the two basal stocks from which each group arose. The true mastodon line is sparsely represented in the fossil drawers of museum collections. *Paleomastodon* dates from about 40 million years ago; then came *Miomastodon* from the Miocene and *Pliomastodon* from the Pliocene some five million years ago. Finally there is the famous American mastodon which was yet another contemporary of modern man.

These four steps from the past to the present seem clear-cut and yet there must be so many intermediate twists and turns which remain hidden, buried beneath tons of geological debris somewhere in the world, that very little is really proven. The fossils available indicate that the true mastodon had its heyday in North America. Indeed it is true that this continent in question has yielded a plethora of fossils which have held the limelight in the study of elephant prehistory for more than a century now, but it is worth remembering that the American mastodon had its origins in another region of the world. The reason for its American fame – and even name – arises from the location of the deposits – large numbers of which have been found. Thus, there could have been mastodons elsewhere, whose remains were not fossilized or whose fossils have not yet been discovered.

During the early eighteenth century some large bones and a few teeth were found around the Hudson and Ohio Rivers. The discoveries were received with little enthusiasm and even a century later were still considered to be of only minor importance. Other remains had been found in 1739 in Big Bone Lake, Kentucky, and it was these and further discoveries that were catapulted to fame in the mid-nineteenth century.

Big Bone Lake was appropriately named. It had once been a huge expanse of open water rich in vegetation. As it became clogged with weed, it was a eutrophy and turned into a thick, soupy bog. Thus, some 25,000 years ago the area was a trap for any creature that ventured too close. Thirsty mastodons, it seems, came in their droves only to be caught, held fast, and sucked under the surface of the treacherous mire. There they lay as

A pack of prehistoric wild dogs moves forward in the hope of snatching a meal, as a doomed mammoth sinks in freezing mud. Such deaths may account for some of the well-preserved mammoths discovered in the Siberian permafrost.

Above: A reconstruction of the woolly mammoth shows it to have been larger than modern elephants, and covered with long, reddish-brown hair. The tusks were longer (up to 16 feet) and curlier than those of today's elephants. Mammoths were widespread in Europe and became extinct only a few thousand years ago.

Above right: Prehistoric proboscidians, classified according to their fossil remains, took many strange forms. Some had tusks in the upper jaw, though not necessarily like those of a modern elephant. Others had tusks in the lower jaw: short, stabbing tusks as in *Phiomia*, or extraordinary great down curved tusks like those of *Deinotherium*.

Right: Vincent Maglio's theory of the evolution of the elphant family is illustrated in this diagram.

7   6   5

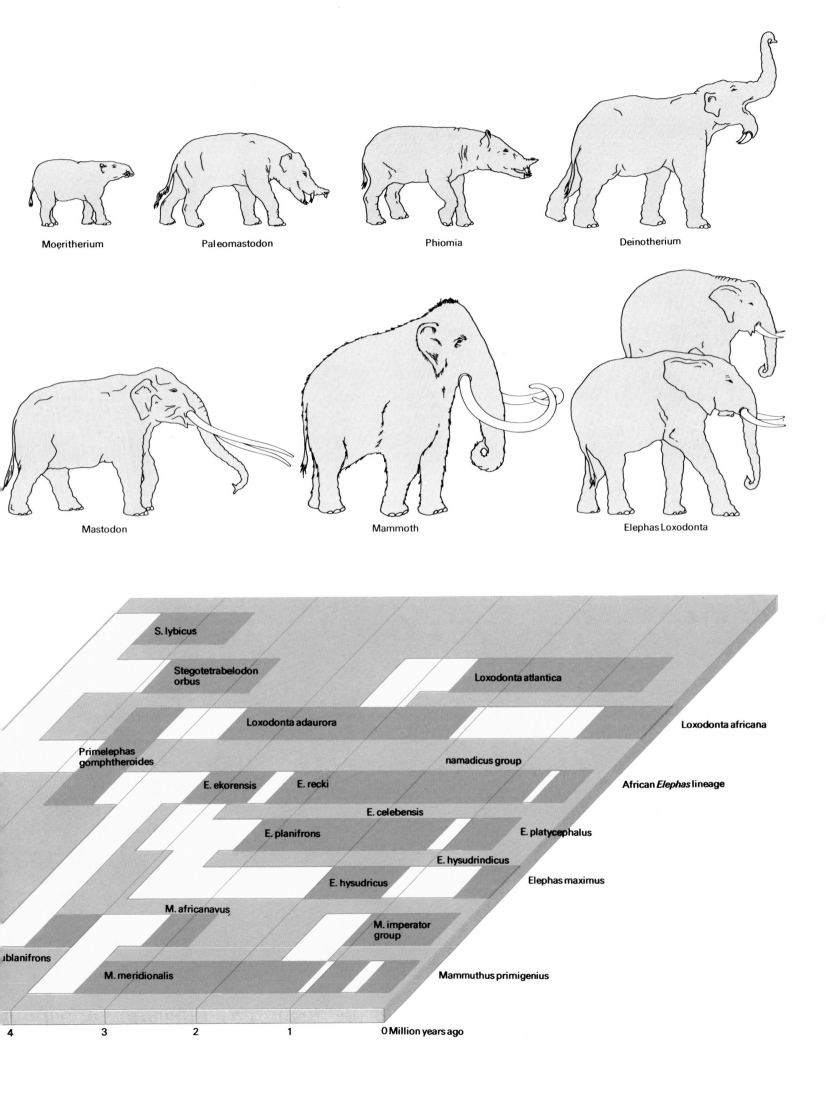

Moeritherium

Paleomastodon

Phiomia

Deinotherium

Mastodon

Mammoth

Elephas Loxodonta

S. lybicus

Stegotetrabelodon orbus

Loxodonta atlantica

Loxodonta adaurora

Loxodonta africana

Primelephas gomphtheroides

namadicus group

African *Elephas* lineage

E. ekorensis

E. recki

E. celebensis

E. platycephalus

E. planifrons

E. hysudrindicus

E. hysudricus

Elephas maximus

M. africanavus

M. imperator group

ublanifrons

M. meridionalis

Mammuthus primigenius

4   3   2   1   0 Million years ago

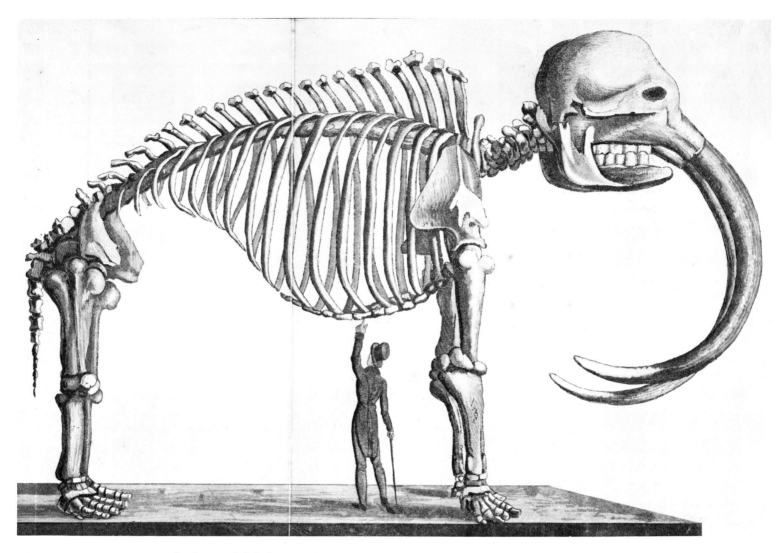

Above: Not least by the shape of its tusks – which seem to have been put in upside-down – one suspects that the artist had not actually seen this mammoth skeleton exhibited at the museum in Philadelphia.

the bog solidified around and within them, preserving them until erosion thousands of years later began to expose them once more. The remains of more than 100 mastodons have so far been found, many of which were retrieved as whole skeletons. From them, highly detailed conclusions can be drawn about the animal's way of life.

It was a big creature, some 15 feet long between tusk and tail and stood at least nine feet at the shoulder. It had a good-sized trunk and the tusks were as much as nine feet long, held forward from the shoulder on a cramped head and not downward as in the modern elephant. It had a dense covering of hair, no doubt a legacy of the ancestral journey across the Bering Straits land-bridge. The major clue to its distant relationship with the living elephants lay in the teeth. Instead of possessing hard ridges, as modern elephant teeth do, they are graced with nipple-shaped projections. It was from this apparently primitive feature alone that Baron Georges Cuvier, the great French zoologist, gave them the name 'mastodon' which simply means, 'nipple tooth.' Primitive or not, these mastodons must have accompanied early man as he too crossed the land-bridge from the Old World into the New.

The proboscidian families so far mentioned – the deinotheres, the gomphotheres and the mastodons – can all be recognized as being very

elephant-like. Yet much closer analysis is necessary to determine which of them could have been the real ancestor of the modern elephant.

Until recently the *Stegodon* was thought to be sufficiently similar to the modern forms to be considered the ancestral stock. (It had presumably broken away from the *Mastodon* – *Trilophodon* lineage some 30 million years ago during the Miocene.) However Vincent Maglio, working from Princeton University in America, has suggested a different pattern of events, based on the evidence of elephant tooth structure. Teeth are a good guide to evolutionary history because they are not only preserved in good condition but they also give valuable clues as the animal's size and feeding habits.

Maglio suggested in 1970 that the elephant's ancestor should be sought among the African gomphotheres, an idea that was endorsed when he examined the remains of *Stegotetrabelodor. syrticus* from the Miocene beds of Syria. The animal had been described in 1941 as no more than a specialized gomphothere. Maglio adopted the view that it was actually better considered a primitive elephant because although its skull was not particularly elephant-like its teeth showed clear indications – not shared with any other proboscidians – of belonging to the elephants of the future. The group to which it belonged lived in Africa some seven million years ago.

The time traveller

This baby mammoth died over 40,000 years ago. She died in a marsh in Siberia, and was preserved by cold at a very fast rate – literally 'fast-frozen' – and was eventually covered by the permafrost, or permanently frozen subsoil. When she was discovered three years ago, in the region of Magadan in eastern Russia, her body was virtually unaffected by decomposition. Almost perfect cells were found in her kidneys and liver, although others were damaged as she thawed out in the laboratory.

Dr Mikhelson, a research scientist at the Soviet Institute of Cytology (study of cells), tried to reproduce a living replica of Dima, using the cells from her internal organs. He claims that but for a laboratory mistake his experiment would have succeeded. Furthermore, he believes that if a cytologist can obtain perfect, deep-frozen cells from a mammoth, that it will be possible to create a 'test-tube' mammoth. The technique involved is that of cloning, the reproduction of living cells from a single parent cell. Dr Mikhelson's plan is to kill the nucleus of a sex cell from a female Indian elephant, and replace it with the mammoth cell. This would then be implanted in a living female elephant which, after a normal gestation period, would give birth, it is hoped, to a live baby mammoth.

Other scientists point out that while research into cloning is advancing rapidly, and structures such as bacteria have been reproduced this way, there is considerable doubt that such a complex creature as a mammoth could be produced – especially from a 'parent' 40,000 years old. In the meantime, Dima has been exhibited in several countries over the world.

Below: Dima, the baby mammoth, as she was seen at the USSR National Exhibition in Earl's Court, London, in 1979.

Mammoth discovery

'In 1846 there was uncommon warm weather in the north of Siberia. Already in May unusual rains poured over the moors and bogs, storms shook the earth, and the streams carried not only ice to the sea, but also large tracts of land, thawed by the masses of warm water fed by the southern rains.... We steamed on the first favorable day up the Indigirka; but there were no thoughts of land. We saw around us only a sea of brown water, and knew the river by the rushing and roaring of the stream....

While we were all quiet, we suddenly heard under our feet a sudden gurgling and stirring, which betrayed the working of the disturbed water. Suddenly our jäger [hunter], ever on the look-out, called loudly, and pointed to a singular and unshapely object, which rose and sank through the disturbed waters. I had already remarked it, but not given it my attention, considering it only drift wood. Now we all hastened to the spot on the shore, had the boat drawn near, and waited until the mysterious thing should again show itself. Our patience was tried, but at last, a black, horrible, giant-like mass was thrust out of the water, and we beheld a colossal elephant's head, armed with mighty tusks, with its long trunk moving in the water, in an unearthly manner, as though seeking for something lost therein. Breathless with astonishment, I beheld the monster hardly twelve feet from me, with his half-open eyes yet showing the whites. It was still in good preservation.

"Mammoth! a Mammoth!" broke out the Tschermomori, and I shouted "Here quickly! chains and ropes!"...

We therefore fastened a rope around his neck, threw a chain round his tusks, that were eight feet long, drove a stake into the ground about 20 feet from the shore, and made chain and rope fast to it. The day went by quicker than I thought for, but still the time seemed long before the animal was secured, as it was only after the lapse of 24 hours that the waters had loosened it. But the position of the animal was interesting to me; it was standing in the earth, and not lying on its side or back as a dead animal naturally would, indicating by this the manner of its destruction. The soft peat or marsh land on which he stepped thousands of years ago gave way by the weight of the giant, and he sank as he stood on it feet foremost, incapable of saving himself, and a severe frost came and turned him into ice, as well as the moor which had buried him; the latter, however, grew and flourished, every summer renewing itself; possibly the neighboring stream had heaped plants and sand over the dead body. God only

From this point onward Maglio recognizes some 25 species of elephants. *Stegotetrabelodon* (two species) gave rise to *Primelephas* (two species) which became a basic stock for the rather primitive *Loxodonta* (two species, one of which survives today as the African elephant) and the more progressive *Elephas* (eleven species, one of which survives today as the Asian elephant). A third branch contained the mammoths.

Of all the Proboscidea, the mammoths were among the most formidable of the prehistoric beasts faced by early man. Indeed, these huge elephants lived well into modern times, dying out only a few thousand years ago at the end of the last ice age. Their remains are still being exhumed in Siberia by the erosive processes of the Arctic Circle, where they were well preserved in ice. The flesh of mammoths has even been eaten by modern scientists and the details of their last meals have been brought under the powerful eye of the modern microscope. For two centuries or more, their remains have been sought by Russians interested in making money from the huge ivory tusks which curled for more than 16 feet from the head.

The story of the first almost complete mammoth ever found concerns a fisherman who was taking some time off from his job to find fragments of ivory washed down toward the sea. From Cassell's *Natural History* we learn how 'a Tungoosian fisherman, named Schumachoff, about the year 1799, was proceeding, as is the custom of fishermen in those parts when fishing proves a failure, along the shores of the Lena in quest of Mammoth tusks, which have been there found in considerable abundance. During his rambles, having gone farther than he had done before, he suddenly came face to face with a huge Mammoth embedded in clear ice. This extraordinary sight seems to have filled him with astonishment and awe; for instead of at once profiting by the fortunate discovery, he allowed several years to roll on before he summoned courage to approach it closely, although it was his habit to make stealthy journeys occasionally to the object of his wonder. At length seeing, it is presumed, that the terrific monster made no signs of eating him up, and that its tusks would bring him a considerable sum of money, he allowed the hope of gain to overcome his superstitious scruples. He boldly broke the barrier of ice, chopped off the tusks, and left the carcase to the mercy of the Wolves and Bears, who, finding it palatable, soon reduced the huge creature to a skeleton. Some two years afterwards a man of science was on the scent, and although so late in at the death, found a huge skeleton with three legs, the eyes still in the orbits, and the brain uninjured in the skull.'

knows what causes had worked for its preservation; now, however, the stream had once more brought it to the light of day, and I, an ephemera of life compared with this primeval giant, was sent here by heaven just at the right time to welcome him.

You can imagine how I jumped for joy.... Picture to yourself an elephant with a body covered with thick fur, about 13 feet in height, and 15 in length, with tusks eight feet long, thick and curving outwards at their ends, a stout trunk of six feet in length, colossal limbs of one foot and a half in thickness, and a tail naked up to the end, which was covered with thick, tufty hair. The animal was fat and well grown; death had overtaken him in the fullness of his powers. His parchment-like, large, naked ears lay fearfully turned up over the head; about the shoulders and the back he had stiff hair, about a foot in length, like a mane. The long outer hair was deep brown and coarsely rooted. The top of the head looked so wild, and was so penetrated with pitch, that it resembled the rind of an old oak-tree. On the sides it was cleaner, and under the outer hair there appeared everywhere a wool, very soft, warm, and thick, and of a yellow brown colour. The giant was well protected against the cold. The whole appearance of the animal was fearfully wild and strange. It had not the shape of our present elephants. As compared with our Indian elephants, its head was rough, the brain case low and narrow, but the trunk and mouth were much larger. The teeth were very powerful. Our elephant is an awkward animal, but compared with this mammoth it is as an Arabian steed to a coarse ugly dray-horse.

I could not divest myself of a feeling of fear as I approached the head; the broken, widely-opened eyes gave the animal an appearance of life, as though it might move in a moment and destroy us with a roar.... The bad smell of the body warned us that it was time to save of it what we could, and the swelling flood, too, bade us to hasten. First of all we cut off the tusks, and sent them to the cutter. Then the people tried to hew the head off, but, notwithstanding their good will, this was slow work. As the belly of the animal was cut open the intestines rolled out, and then the smell was so dreadful that I could not overcome my nauseousness, and was obliged to turn away. But I had the stomach separated and brought on one side. It was well filled, and the contents instructive and well preserved. The principal were of young shoots of the fir and pine; a quantity of young fir cones also, in a chewed state, were mixed with the mass.'

Benkendorf

An artist's impression of the discovery of the mammoth by Schumachoff on the banks of the River Lena in Siberia, 1799. The beast (which was actually encased in ice) appears to have just stepped out from behind a cliff, to the slight surprise of the passing fisherman.

The climax of a prehistoric mammoth hunt. One archeological site in Czechoslovakia contained bones from about 900 mammoths.

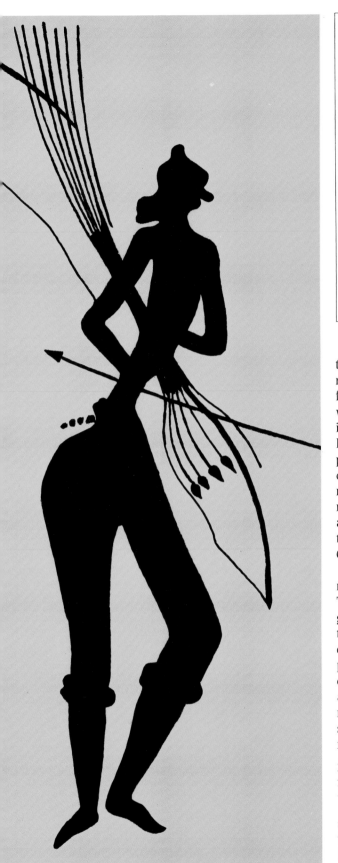

Prehistoric men — such as the hunter painted on a cave wall in Teruel, Spain (above) — hunted mammoths, and painted them in cave shelters. These mammoth paintings are from sites in France and Spain. The two rock engravings from the Central Sahara (near left: center and bottom), made about 4000 years ago, show that the Sahara became a desert only in comparatively recent times; previously it was as green and full of wild animals as East Africa was before the white man came.

Mammoth definitions

'Some authors derive the name "Mammoth" from the word *Behemoth*, used in the book of Job to designate an immensely large animal, or from *Mehemoth*, an Arab term applied to elephants of extraordinary size; while others are of opinion that it is merely an adoption of the word *Mammouth*, given by the Siberians to a huge animal, which they (in order to account for the quantity of Mammoth-horns, or fossil ivory) pretend lived underground in the manner of moles, and could not bear the light of day.'

from *A Popular Dictionary of Animated Nature*, 1878.

Such a discovery was met with incredulity in the Western world, although the bones were as much as one might have expected from a good fossil find. It was not until 1846 that the scientific world was stunned with the news of a completely intact mammoth find. Apparently a young Russian engineer called Benkendorf was employed by his government to help survey the coast of the mouth of the Lena and Indigirka rivers and made his discovery as he progressed up the latter river in a small iron steam-cutter. His own account of the exciting events that followed is translated from a letter he later wrote to a friend in Germany (see box, pages 18–19).

Such remains as these are remarkable for reasons other than their state of preservation. They show that the elephant family which had its gomphothere origins in Africa, produced species that were able to radiate to, and flourish in, the coldest regions of the earth. The mammoth complex, in which there were some seven species, was one of the more successful of recent proboscidians and it is well represented in cave paintings of early man in France and Spain. It originated from the same *Primelephas* stock that gave rise to the modern genus *Elephas* which also migrated from Africa – more than once – to colonize much of Europe and Asia. The modern genus *Loxodonta* has never left Africa.

We will never really know why they went into such a decline and to what extent humans were the cause of it during their own brief history. Many hold the view that a million or so years ago man's influence was still too localized to have set them off on the road to evolutionary decline. By the time man was beginning to alter the ecology of the world to suit himself regardless of the consequences to other forms of wildlife, the great elephant family was already past its peak and sliding toward extinction. All that remains are the subspecies of *Loxodonta africana* in Africa and the handful of subspecies of *Elephas indicus* from Southeast Asia.

2:THE LIVING ELEPHANT

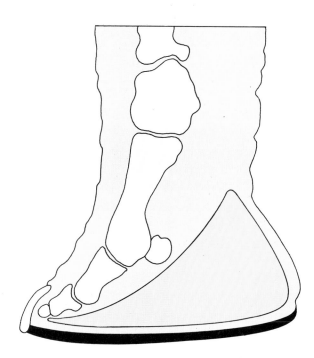

Many millions of years have been 'invested' in producing the modern-day elephant, whether it lives in Africa or in India, in forest or in open woodland. It may look cumbersome, but it is superbly equipped to survive and reproduce in equatorial conditions.

The tropics are characterized by alternating periods of drought and intense rains. The elephant cannot change itself to meet the requirements of each particular seasonal demand, so it must present to the world a body which can tolerate the worst average conditions that each period of the year has to offer. (In bad years, of course, when the extremes go way beyond this average expectancy, the animals will suffer enormously. The famous East African droughts of 1961 and 1970 killed several thousand elephants who would otherwise have survived quite comfortably.)

Within the ecological framework of survival and reproduction – two aspects which inevitably involve interactions *between* elephants – there is the individual itself. At its full height, the shoulder of a mature bull African elephant will tower to as much as 13 feet and the accompanying weight on sturdy limbs may be as much as six tons.

It is not surprising that an animal which has evolved to such a size has also had to equip itself with other anatomical peculiarities. Feet, legs, nose, ears, and teeth all operate in a peculiarly elephantine way to ease the tasks of walking, feeding, drinking, and keeping cool.

The whole foreleg from shoulder to nail is an amazing structure. It may be held as straight as a column of steel to give long, vertical support. In ancient times, before the elephant was kept in

The diagram above shows the structure of an elephant's foot. The bones are so arranged that the elephant virtually walks on tiptoe: hence its capacity for delicate movement. The foot is cushioned, and the elephant's weight distributed, by a thick fatty pad inside the sole of the foot (below). The African bush elephant has four toenails on the front feet and three on the back; the Asian has five and four respectively.

captivity or observed at close quarters for any length of time, it was generally accepted that the powerful limbs were totally devoid of joints. There is a certain stiff-leggedness which accompanies the normal, ambling gait of the elephant, and the idea of one bone running the entire length of the leg caught on to such an extent that Shakespeare alluded to it in his play *Troilus and Cressida*. Ulysses, commenting on Ajax's rather inflexible attitude toward Achilles, remarks, 'The Elephant hath joints, but none for courtesy. His legs are legs for necessity, not for flexure.' Yet the limbs are also oddly flexible, appearing at times to possess an extra joint. This, of course, is an illusion. There is a shoulder, knee (or elbow), an ankle (or wrist), and digits comparable to those of other mammals. The peculiarity concerns the ankle, which is set much further back along the length of the limb. Thus it takes the position of a joint almost half-way between the knee and where one might expect the ankle to be.

There is a second feature of the elephant limb which demands special attention. It is that elephants walk virtually on tiptoe. However contradictary to their weight this may seem, it is not only true but also an ingenious means of enabling the foot to act as a cushion, softening the blow of every step. The bones of the toe actually point toward the ground, but their position is not outwardly visible. They are embedded in elasticated fibers which are themselves held fast within large quantities of fatty tissue. The whole collection of bones, fibers and fats are held in shape by the thick outer covering of the elephant's body on which the hooves, the equivalent of nails, are located. Their position corresponds approximately to the position of the finger and toe bones beneath the surface, although they are not attached to them. These hooves may be very small and are sometimes torn off during the normal passage of life. The number present on each foot should not, as has previously happened, be used as a means of identifying different subspecies of elephant. Thus, at the end of each of the elephant's legs there is a compressible, shock-absorbing pad which, because of its sponge-like qualities, is able to expand and contract when the weight of its owner is alternately lowered and raised upon it. Its stabilizing qualities also render it highly adaptable to any unevenness in the ground. Steep inclines and rocky terrains can be negotiated with silent ease because each pad adjusts itself independently to the immediate requirements of a sure foothold.

Even in the dead of night the foot may be used as a highly sensitive organ of touch. One of the unforgettable experiences of the African bush is to be awoken in a flimsy tent when a herd of elephants moves in to browse among the trees in and around the campsite.

When this happened to me for the first time – in Tanzania in 1972 – my immediate reaction to their powerful presence (betrayed only by the curious rumblings they make with the larynx) was of impending doom. I was convinced that one of them would soon blunder carelessly into the numerous guy-ropes that had been stretched out like trip-wires and that in the ensuing panic our meager canvas protection would be bulldozed to the ground, but suddenly calm prevailed. It was obvious that the elephants were so close that they must actually be stepping over the taut ropes that stood in their way. Occasionally a corner of the tent would vibrate sharply as a guy-rope was investigated by trunk or foot. In such meticulous fashion, five enormous shadows threaded their way through the campsite and continued along the river bank.

Below: There is some cause for alarm as an elephant dwarfs the author's tent in Tanzania in 1972, but no damage was done.

Above: The normal walking pace of an elephant is about 6mph; at a fast rolling walk it may reach 15mph. A charging elephant can attain 18mph but only for a short distance.

owner quite well as an organ of smell and little else. Whether an animal such as the *Moeritherium* really was a direct ancestor of modern elephants will be debated for years to come, but nonetheless, the ancestor we are looking for here would have been of such a small size that it would have been trunkless in the sense that we accept today. Its head would have been sufficiently small and close to the ground that it could have been lifted and dropped with ease, with the teeth making direct contact with the vegetation on which it fed.

However it seems that these early elephant types were to develop along an evolutionary pathway of increasing size. As the bulkier head that resulted from the process was lifted higher off the ground, it became more important that strong muscles evolved to hold it closer to the body skeleton. Simply to lengthen the neck, as has happened in the smaller-headed and differently shaped giraffe, was not mechanically possible for an animal of elephant-like proportions.

By about 35 million years ago, the trial and error processes of mutation and natural selection seem to have provided a number of possible answers to how this type of animal was going to reach its food from the ground. Two types of creature, called 'spoon-tuskers' and 'shovel-tuskers,' grew an extended lower jaw. Above this was an extended upper lip which could rake off and shovel toward the throat any food collected in the jaw immediately below it. This sort of food-gathering mechanism would have worked only if the animals lived in, or close to, water where weeds could be scooped up or where the large teeth could be forced easily into soft mud. These early elephant-types, it is presumed, were essentially swamp-bound. *Moeritherium*, their possible ancestor, was almost certainly a water-dwelling animal more akin in its behavior to the present-day hippopotamus than to the elephant. At some stage in the subsequent evolution of the trunk there must have been a move to dry land where the successful swamp technique was of little use. Over successive generations, spanning millions of years, the lower jaw receded further and the trunk elongated. It acquired more uses, and increased the chances of survival. Thus, two million years ago, the lower jaw had been almost entirely disposed of as a projection and the trunk had elongated to such an extent that *Stegomastodon* showed the facial proportions of a twentieth century elephant. The last million or so years provided the finishing touches to a multipurpose organ. It deserves closer attention if it is to be better understood.

The elephant's trunk is essentially a combined elongation of the nose and the upper lip. The only significant difference between the African and the Asian species is that the former has two small projections at the tip of its trunk – one above and

For centuries the elephant has been ridiculed because of its trunk. 'A tail at the front' is the popular image of this long and heavy proboscis. However a tail is not a region of the body readily associated with dexterity, sensitivity, or brute force. These are but a few of the remarkable attributes of the elephant's trunk. It is such a significant feature that the name of the order to which elephants belong, the Proboscidea, denotes this feature in particular.

It is worth having a look at how this trunk – which is really none other than an elongated nose – developed into its present form and function. About 60 million years ago the ancestor of the modern elephant was a small creature which did not possess a trunk at all. Its nose was probably a large fleshy affair but it would have served its one below – while the latter has only the one above. The trunk quite literally serves as a fifth limb and its degree of flexibility – it has no bones in it – is apparently at odds with the rest of the elephant's massive inflexibility. Such a solid, heavy body would hardly survive unless it was equipped with some efficient means of satisfying its daily needs of food and water intake. The trunk fills the need admirably. It plucks leaves and branches growing high up on trees and grass from the ground, and stuffs them all into its small, fleshy mouth below the base of the trunk. Water is sucked up and then squirted into its throat a gallon or more at a time.

There are many other functions for which the trunk is employed. One must not lose sight of the fact that, whatever its shape and most obvious uses, it is still basically a nose. The nostrils are located at the very tip, as much as eight feet from the head, and run the entire length of the trunk. They are divided along their length by a fleshy partition, the septum. The thousands of separate muscles that are woven around these internal tubes allow the trunk to be twisted and turned through any number of contortions to test the air for scents of neighboring elephants or potential predators. This is an invaluable asset because the elephant's eyesight is not particularly good. The length of the trunk enables it not only to be cast around through a wide arc in search of airborne

Below: Asian elephants extend their trunks like siphons to reach water that has not been muddied by their feet. A small baby elephant, at front, though nearly submerged, bravely imitates its elders.

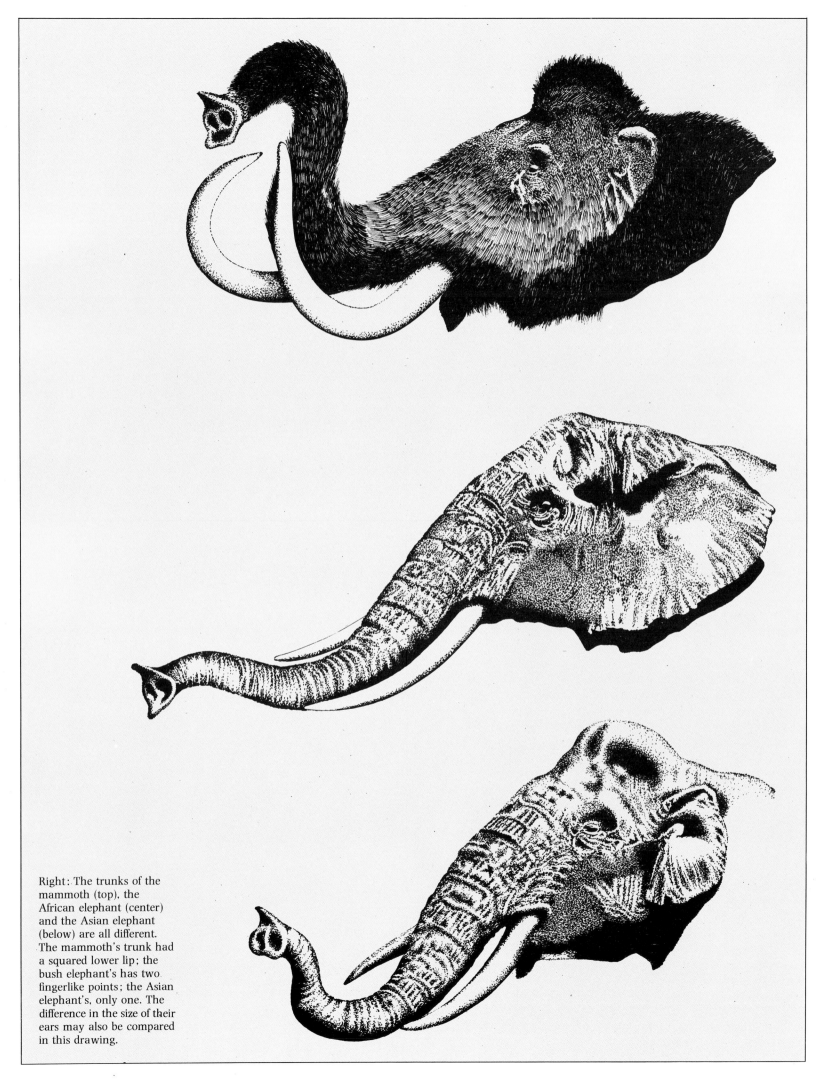

Right: The trunks of the mammoth (top), the African elephant (center) and the Asian elephant (below) are all different. The mammoth's trunk had a squared lower lip; the bush elephant's has two fingerlike points; the Asian elephant's, only one. The difference in the size of their ears may also be compared in this drawing.

Left above and below: The skull of an elephant is massive enough to support the tusks and provide plenty of surface for the attachment of big muscles. To keep it light it is filled with cavities or sinuses, like a bony sponge. The ivory of the tusks (a form of dentine) covers a pulpy inner core which, like a human tooth nerve, is extremely sensitive if exposed.

Right: Combining its considerable intelligence and flexible trunk, a baby elephant in the zoo has learned how to turn on the tap and help itself to a drink.

messages, but also to be held high above thick vegetation where the passage of the wind is neither interrupted nor strongly infused with smells from a lower level.

Wind may also be expelled forcibly *from* the trunk to produce noises of varying pitch and intensity, and becomes an organ of communication. Soft, pleasurable squeaks of greeting are used between individuals and harsh 'trumpeting' sounds are blasted out as a warning to any other animal approaching too close for comfort. It is a warning to be heeded for, once committed to its charge, an adult elephant, with its sensitive trunk curled up for protection, can outrun a man in open country and will vent its fury on a large vehicle, reducing it to scrap metal in a matter of minutes.

In the heat of the tropical day, most animals are driven to find shade under bushes or trees. The elephant is no exception to this rule, but its trunk

Left: Another example of ingenuity in getting a drink: elephants on this Kenyan ranch have learned to reach over the top of the household water tank and steal water.

Left: An adult elephant, like Ahmed, Kenya's famous old tusker, drinks more than 30 gallons of water a day, 1.5 gallons in each trunkful.

An elephant raises its trunk to scent the wind. Its eyesight is poor, but the senses of hearing (aided by forward-turned ears) and smell are good.

acts as an extra cooling device. It can lose heat through the large surface area of the trunk's skin and can also use the trunk to spray showers of water over its body. It may stand for hours in a water hole, alternately squirting water into its mouth or over its rough hide. An elephant in very deep water may even use its trunk as a snorkel with, occasionally, just the last few air-breathing inches projecting above the surface. The trunk may also be used to spray clouds of dust over the body when flies and other external irritants are proving troublesome.

Perhaps, to the human observer at least, the most remarkable attribute of the trunk is its combination of brute strength and fingertip sensitivity. It is awe inspiring to watch the same organ that wraps itself around a fallen tree and hauls it roughly out of the way turn its attention toward a single, delicate leaf on another tree and then pluck it without causing more than a ripple of agitation across the rest of the branch. It is this same delicacy of touch which elephants employ when they caress each other. Their relationships are strong and when two individuals meet their trunks feel each other before intertwining in a display of mutual affection.

Anyone who has seen elephants in zoos or circuses can immediately identify the African or Asian species by the size and shape of their ears. There are, of course, many other differences between them – the trunk tip, the tusks, and the shape of the body are the more obvious ones – but the ears remain the most popular diagnostic feature to most people. Both types of elephant have very good hearing, which suggests that for

Below: An elephant extends its trunk – as delicate, flexible and precise as the arm and hand of the girl offering a morsel of food.

Above: In the Indian Army, elephants were trained to raise their trunks in unison as a gesture of salute, as seen in this engraving c1871 of Dinapore, India.

Keeping cool

Like any other mammal, the elephant must keep its body temperature within a limited range if it is not to die. Cold is rarely a problem within the geographical range of wild elephants, but heat is another matter. The elephant's slow metabolism means that its body does not gain heat quickly, and the thick skin acts as an insulator to maintain an even internal temperature. There is also some evidence to suggest that an elephant can permit a much higher body temperature than any other mammal, without apparent ill effects. There are sweat glands over the body which aid heat loss over the huge surface area.

The most important thermoregulation device, however, is the elephant's ear. The thin skin covers a network of blood vessels, allowing blood to lose heat to the air at a considerable rate. (Iain Douglas-Hamilton recorded a drop of more than 16 degrees Fahrenheit in the temperature of blood that had just passed through the ears of an African elephant.)

To increase the efficiency of its ears, the elephant flaps them almost constantly to encourage cool air currents around its head. The ears are also sprayed with water by the trunk whenever possible. During the hottest part of the day elephants rest in the shade; and frequent, lengthy baths are another excellent – and evidently enjoyable – way of keeping cool.

Left: An elephant takes a dust shower to cool itself down and discourage parasites.

Above: Elephants are excellent swimmers and enter even deep water with evident enjoyment, using their trunks as snorkels.

Above: An elephant endures midday heat by resting immobile in the shade, fanning its ears to create a blood-cooling breeze.

Above: Slapping on a cooling mud pack: in Tsavo National Park, Kenya, most elephants are stained bright red by the native clay soil.

Right: A baby elephant abandons itself to the pleasure of a good soak.

Below: Disturbed while taking a shower, an African bull elephant signals alarm by raising his tail and spreading his ears.

The elephant's trunk must be one of the most versatile limbs in creation. It is used for smelling; gathering food; sucking up water; spraying water, dust, or mud; carrying, pushing or pulling operations; protecting and controlling the young; and touching – for identification or communication. A common recognition signal is for one elephant to put its trunk tip just inside the mouth of another.

Above: Different head shape, ear size, and number of toenails distinguish the African bush elephant (left) from the Asian elephant (right). A full-grown bush elephant is the largest, a bull reaching 11 feet or more, while the Asian elephant rarely exceeds 10 feet. The African forest elephant (opposite, above left) is the smallest, at 7 to 8 feet.

their different requirements each has ears of a size well suited to its particular needs. It may be tempting to assume that the African elephant's much larger ears give it better hearing, but this is not true. The discrepancy indicates an alternative explanation – that certain organs have more than one function. In this respect the larger ears of the African elephant have several very important roles to fulfill.

The basic role of the ear is to detect sounds and convey them to the brain. The external portion of the ear, the flap or pinna, receives sound waves which are then passed as vibrations through the bones of the inner ear. Messages are sent to the brain where they are interpreted accordingly. The discrepancy between the two species arises only at the external section of the ear – the flap itself. Why should the ears agree on internal structure and disagree so remarkably on external proportions? The answer must have something to do with where and how they live.

The small-eared Asian elephant is essentially a forest dweller occupying a region with a fairly well defined seasonal climate some way north of the equator. Its ear flaps are small. The large-eared African elephant, by contrast, lives on the equator over part of its range and occupies open, sun-drenched savannah country. The smaller, forest-bound African elephant, *Loxodonta africana cyclotis* has proportionally smaller ears than its large savannah counterpart *Loxodonta africana africana*. Thus, there seems to be some correlation between ear size and exposure to the sun. The elephant of the savannah naturally has less shelter from the heat of the equator than does its counterpart of the forest. For this reason it must make every effort to keep its body cool.

The large surface area of the ear flaps act as the most important external organ of body heat control. On the underside of each ear there is an extensive, fan-like arrangement of blood vessels running just below the surface of the skin. During the hottest time of the day these vessels are fully extended as blood from the warm depths of the elephant's body flows through them. The blood quickly loses its heat to the air around it and is then returned to the body where it will collect more unwanted warmth for transportation to the

Above: The African forest elephant has a slim head, rounder ears, and long, slender tusks.

Above: Elephants rarely live more than 60 years.

Above: Rembrandt van Rijn's charcoal sketch of an Asian elephant accurately depicts both the anatomy and personality of the animal.

ear. The whole process is accelerated by the elephant flapping its ears forward and back so that the undersides are continually exposed to the air. Without this cooling mechanism, the African elephant of the open bush would run the risk of overheating internally, with possibly fatal results. There is evidence to suggest that if an elephant loses the ability to bring its ears into the forward position, it may suffer cooling problems for the rest of its life.

During the course of its life, an elephant will inevitably lose pieces out of its large flaps, either through fighting or in natural accidents. Although these may leave them ragged and torn, the damage will not affect the heat regulation process as long as the muscles controlling the movement of the whole ear are not impaired. The ears, whose basic function is to detect sounds, have therefore evolved to provide a vital survival process.

Beyond this, the ears have another use of paramount importance. One of the ways in which many animals can increase their apparent size, particularly during threat displays, is to make use of their body covering or appendages in such a way that they appear more formidable than they are. This type of display, which has evolved because animals that save energy by not fighting tend to outlive their more aggressive fellows, depends upon the external features of the animal and the ways in which they can best be used to intimidate a potential enemy (perhaps an individual of an unrelated species) or a potential rival. Typically, a bird will raise its feathers, a lizard may erect a large, brightly colored frill around its head, and a toad may gulp down air to swell the size of its body. An African elephant extends its ears.

From a distance, these ears may not seem so very large, especially as seen in relation to the body size of the elephant. However, when seen close to and head on, with the body largely obscured, they can be used to devastating effect. When they are held forward at about 90 degrees to the rest of the body they are seen in their full enormity. They may treble the width of the elephant's head, framing and exaggerating the power of the gleaming, forward-pointing ivory tusks. Each ear may be more than six feet long and three feet wide – enough to wrap itself quite comfortably around an average human being. When the dust beneath the agitated feet is pounded into a frenzied cloud, the vision of towering strength is truly the most awe inspiring, if not the most terrifying, of animal spectacles. There is still one more aspect of the elephant's head which is worthy of consideration: the teeth. These are unusual not only for the development of upper incisors into the tusks but also because they effectively determine an elephant's lifespan.

Above: An adult elephant, such as this one browsing on thorny acacia, eats several hundred pounds of food a day. Inefficient chewing and digestion, however, means that only about 45 percent of this is digested.

Right: An elephant's tusks grow throughout its life, but wear and damage prevent them from reaching their potential length. Often an elephant uses one tusk more than the other, being 'right- or left-handed' like a human. The 'master tusk' is usually shorter and worn smoother than the other.

All elephants have tusks, except for the Sumatran subspecies. They are more noticeable in the African species in which they grow to a large size visible in both sexes. In the Asian species, it is only the males whose tusks are readily visible and even these are much smaller than those of their African relatives. These tusks are part of the normal dentition of elephants. They are modified teeth whose function has changed dramatically from the more normal cutting, tearing, or chewing roles within the animal's mouth. They are incisors (not canines, the more traditional fangs) growing out from the upper jaw and they have no counterpart in the lower jaw. Canine teeth are entirely absent in both jaws, leaving no more than four sets of molars – one in each jaw – to do all the work of chewing and grinding the many tons of vegetation that pass into the elephant's stomach during its lifetime.

Elephants are born with so-called 'milk' tusks which are only a few centimeters long and are replaced by permanent tusks after about a year. These latter tusks are made of ivory – a resilient mixture of dentine and cartilage coated with calcium. The durability of the compound has been exploited by man the world over for centuries and is one of the major reasons for the tragic decline in elephant numbers since the advent of *Homo sapiens* (see Chapter 6).

From the first year of their eruption, the permanent tusks continue to grow. The activity of special cells within them controls the rate at which they increase their length and girth. This rate varies between individuals and between the sexes. Thus, in the African elephant, the tusks of the male not only increase in weight faster than those of the female but are also more robust and more widely spaced. Tusks may be chipped and broken as a result of wear and tear, for they are used in a great many ways, including fighting and digging, which subject them to enormous stress. However in general the tusks survive intact and it is the process of perpetual growth which so easily distinguishes an aging elephant from the middle-aged and young around it. An old male African elephant may under exceptional circumstances

Below: A wary elephant turns its huge ears forward like sails in threat display.

Above: The dominant female, or matriarch, of a group is usually the first to threaten an intruder, such as the photographer.

Elephant charge!

Faced with an intruder, the matriarch (above) or leading bull of an elephant group usually comes to the fore and threatens – head and tail held high, ears spread wide to increase the apparent size of an already daunting animal (left above). It may also trumpet, and stamp up dust from the earth. This display is often followed up by a charge (left below). It may be a 'dummy' charge – not followed through by attack – but it is terrifying enough to make most intruders retreat at speed.

As many people have learned to their cost, a dummy charge can suddenly become the real thing. Or, as Iain Douglas-Hamilton discovered with the four female elephants he named the Terrible Torone Sisters, an elephant may charge without any warning. When an elephant does attack, it can cause terrible damage. Vehicles may be tusked, trampled, and rolled to a mangled wreck. Human beings have been tossed, gored, and trampled to death; only recently a British television cameraman was killed by the subject of his film. Photographers and tourists are wise to watch from a strong and fast motor vehicle – six tons of intelligent, mobile aggression are not to be taken lightly.

carry tusks as much as three meters in length and weighing over 200lb each. The solid head and sturdy neck, which increases its muscle power as the tusks increase in length and weight, is well able to withstand the strain imposed by these magnificently overgrown teeth, which are embedded into the skull for as much as a third of their length.

There is, however, a lot more to an elephant's teeth than its tusks. Those housed within the small mouth are themselves a wonder of evolution – not so much for what they are and for how they function but more for the manner in which they appear and for the consequences this has for the elephant's ultimate survival. In both Asian and African elephants, the more usual mammalian tooth pattern is discarded. Gone are the nipping frontal incisors and the adjacent tearing canines. The upper incisors remain as tusks, which play only a minor role in food gathering and no role at all in preparing the food for swallowing. In the mouth itself, only the molars remain. So one must note that elephants – like many other herbivores – are highly inefficient at digesting their food. Something like 45 percent of their vegetation intake passes straight through the system. They need to eat for up to 16 hours, and often longer, every day to take in the several hundredweight of greenery from which they will extract enough nutrients to satisfy their bulky needs.

This method of nutrition, of course, places a special burden on the teeth and it is clear that if an elephant were equipped with a full set of permanent teeth early in life, the teeth would very soon be worn down to the gums. With regard to the teeth, evolution has provided a formula which enables the elephant to chew its way through several decades of life and dooms it only when it has reproduced.

The system works as follows: the elephant is equipped with broad, flat molars which occupy the left and right sides of both upper and lower jaws. Each of these four areas will accommodate six molars, giving a total of 24 in all. They do not appear all together, but replace each other in series. Each set of teeth lasts for a few years and as they wear out and flake off, they are replaced from behind by the next set. The following teeth are always larger than the ones from which they take over, so that tooth size keeps pace with the expanding jaw.

The newborn elephant has eight teeth, for the first and second molars are already in place at the time of its birth. The first of these is nearly two inches long and the second immediately behind it is twice the size. After three or four years, the first molar has not only been ground down but has moved forward into contact with the jaw bone. It now flakes off in distinct layers (*lamellae*). The second molar continues to move forward until it

Above: The elephant's nose and upper lip has evolved into a trunk; the lower lip is soft and fleshy. The tongue and mouth lining are soft and pink. An elephant has no canine teeth; its incisors have been modified into tusks.

assumes a dominant role which will last for a further three or four years. By this time, at about seven years of age, the third molar is growing in each of the four places on the jaws. It becomes fully functional at anything up to 13 years of age and remains so until the fourth molar is in complete use by the time the elephant reaches its twenty-fifth year. The overlapping growth and wear process means that at this stage the fifth molar has already erupted, although it will not be in a full working position until at least another 15 or 20 years have passed. At this point our elephant will be in its mid-forties and in the prime of life, by which time it should have made its vital contribution to the next generation.

Now it has only one more set of teeth to come. Before the fifth molar is fully functional, the sixth and final molar – which measures up to 10 inches along its grinding surface – is well under way. An animal in its fiftieth year will be on its last teeth. Thus, its days of healthy feeding are coming to an end. As the tooth wears down and flakes away leaving an empty space behind it, the elephant becomes less and less efficient at feeding. Gradually, the food eaten must be more lush and capable of being more easily chewed. Such food is not abundant generally, and as the elephant begins to suffer from malnutrition it wanders in search of its special requirements and breaks away from the herd. Death is not too far away. Once the teeth have gone, the animal is irrever-

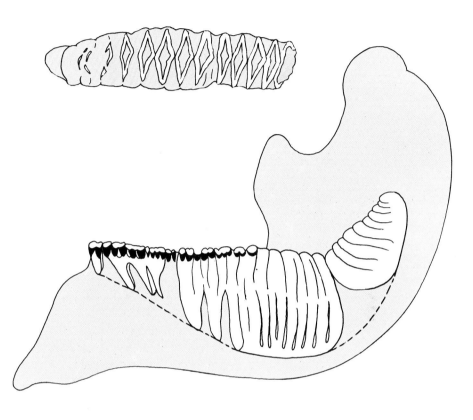

Above: The elephant's huge molars, up to a foot long and 8lb in weight, consist of upright plates of dentine in a block of bony cementum. The tops of the dentine plates form characteristic ridges as they are ground down by chewing (above). As a tooth ages a new and larger one grows behind it (below) and eventually replaces it. Twenty-four teeth – six in each half of each jaw – are formed during the elephant's life.

Left: Study of elephant jawbones, as at the Tsavo National Park Research Center, yields valuable scientific data.

Above: Flashing the giant tusks that earned his fame, Ahmed descends forested Mount Marsabit to drink in a lake.

The grand old man

Above: Ahmed's inelegantly stuffed body is now displayed at Nairobi Museum, Kenya.

Ahmed, the great old tusker of Mount Marsabit in Kenya, was declared a living national monument by President Kenyatta, and provided with a constant guard against poachers. He was one of the few elephants to be known to many more people than those who actually saw him, for he was elusive, a loner who had occasional amicable encounters with other elephants during his forest wanderings. While he was alive his tusks were estimated to be of record size, but when he died – aged 55, in 1974 – his tusks were found to weigh 148lb each: no mean size but far from exceptional. His enjoyment of a daily bath in a lake can be appreciated from the photograph of him on page 33. After his death his body was stuffed and placed on display at the Nairobi Museum (above).

sibly left to a process of degeneration. Most die around the age of 60, others may live until they are well into their seventies.

It is a biological process that on closer inspection reveals a genetically controlled system which works well under the existing conditions of life. The successful individual has made its contribution to both its generation and those to come. It cannot, perhaps it should not, live any longer than is necessary, because its continued existence means that food and space are denied to others of a younger age. Thus, the aging elephant is detached from the crowd to pass its remaining years in isolation.

Ahmed, the grand old tusker from Mount Marsabit in northern Kenya, was such an animal. While he was alive his huge tusks were estimated to be the largest ever known from that region of Africa. It was not until his natural death occurred in 1974 that the tusks could be tested on the scales. They weighed no more than 296lb together. By comparison with others – the heaviest weighed 440lb – this is paltry. However there was something special about Ahmed as he ambled laboriously through the cloud forest of his isolated mountain, protected in his final declining years from poachers by a constant guard, and declared a national monument by the late President Kenyatta himself.

Above: The ears of elephants vary considerably in shape, often bearing holes or tears. Together with tusk shape, this makes identification of individual elephants in the wild comparatively easy.

Left: When peacefully browsing, elephants make noises often described as 'tummy-rumbling' which maintain contact with other members of the group. This unusual sound is now known to be produced in the elephant's larynx and may be likened to purring! If elephants are alarmed the rumbling ceases immediately.

3: LIVING WILD

There are two popular images of elephants in the wild. One is of creatures living socially in family groups. The other – the subject of many adventure stories – is of the lone individual, the 'rogue' elephant, bad-tempered, threatening, and vengeful.

In fact, the lone elephant is something of a rarity in the wild. Only under exceptional circumstances will an individual break away from other elephants and lead a solitary life. Interestingly, the animals that do break away from the herd tradition are nearly always males. The factors contributing to this special behavior can be varied. As we have already seen in the previous chapter, the decay of the molar teeth forces them to remain close to lush vegetation while the other elephants wander to feed more freely elsewhere. Old age may leave an elephant crippled with arthritis and leave it unable to maintain the speed required to keep up with the rest of the herd.

However attractive these arguments may seem, it is difficult to see why they should apply to males more than females. Both are equally susceptible to either condition, which is more a function of years than of sex. The real answer to this behavioral trait must lie elsewhere, perhaps even in the realms of individual personality acting in combination with such aspects as those mentioned above. Individual animals, like humans, vary as much in their characters and their moods as much as in their physical attributes. However female elephants are crucial to the welfare of group structure – particularly where the young are concerned – and the movements of the herds may well be adapted to the condition of an aging cow because despite her advanced years and possibly cantankerous nature, she still has an important role to play in elephant society.

Males, by contrast, take little or no responsibility in educating or protecting the youngsters and when they are afflicted by the crippling characteristics of senility, they may simply be left to fend for themselves. Without social ties to hold them back or to encourage concessions to be made on their behalf the males may depart at any time, more or less according to their personal whims.

Whatever the reasons for these apparent banishments, these animals tend to live out their remaining days in solitary peace. Occasionally, however, they become so bad-tempered and aggressive that they will attack any intruder on sight or even terrorize sections of the bush, causing extensive damage to ground that has been cultivated by man. It is to these particularly unfriendly and potentially dangerous individuals that the tag 'rogue' elephant is applied. It may be surprising to learn that not only are very few individuals worthy of such a label but that it is also a condition more commonly found in the Asian elephant than in the African, although the latter species is more associated with ferocity.

The typical 'rogue' – a term that should not be applied casually to every lone elephant – is almost certainly suffering in some way. It may be that old age has sent it slightly mad or it may be that it has incurred an injury which causes continued aggravation, keeping the poor creature in a constant state of pain and nervous tension which is released only by furious assaults on any obstacle – human or otherwise – that catches its eye. In his book, written in 1878, *Thirteen Years Among the Beasts of India*, George Sanderson tells of an Asian elephant which patrolled several miles of jungle road near Mysore. Its initial mock-charges at travellers suddenly turned into full-blooded assaults which could have ended fatally. Sanderson took it upon himself to rid the terror-stricken people of the menace which was so violently disrupting their lives. When he finally tracked down and killed his quarry, he found that the elephant had somehow lost most of its tail and that the remaining portion was festering so badly that it was obviously the cause of the madness with which the unfortunate animal had been possessed.

Despite the impact that these conspicuous animals make upon human societies, their behavior is the exception to the rule. The normal state is of carefully age-structured groups living peacefully under the dominance of a single, experienced female. She, the epitome of power and control, is referred to as the matriarch.

Elephants require a colossal intake of food and water each day. The vegetation on which they live is composed largely of cellulose which their digestive juices are very inefficient at breaking down within their bodies. However, this foodstuff contains only small amounts of proteins and other vital life-sustaining chemicals. As a result, the food must be consumed at a constant rate and when the useful elements have been extracted from it, the undigested waste must be eliminated quickly to make room for the next load. So elephants eat virtually nonstop, for up to 16 hours a day. Because they are almost without predators, they feed both by day and night. They must, of course, sleep sometimes, but they can manage with short, accumulative dozes. Occasionally, they will drop off as they stand upright, just for a few minutes. During the day, they may seek out a shady spot under a tree and lie down for an hour or so unless disturbed. Three or four hours a day seem to provide them with ample rest – a recuperative system that has evolved around the number of hours that must be devoted to feeding.

The eating habits of elephants offer a convenient theme with which to begin an investigation of group structures. Feeding is an activity that all elephants must perform all of their lives – an elephant living for 65 years will have spent something like 45 of those years feeding – so it

Right: Old male elephants often live a very solitary existence. They are usually peaceful unless provoked; but occasionally one may become aggressive and earn itself the title of rogue elephant.

Below: Elephants usually browse in groups of about a dozen closely related animals, led by a dominant female or matriarch. Groups browsing close to each other are usually members of the same large family.

Above: Much of the elephant's usual foodstuff is composed of indigestible cellulose fiber —another reason why it needs to eat so much.

Right: In order to consume enough food elephants must spend at least 16 hours of each day just eating.

Left: The range of an adult
African bush elephant may
vary from about 20 square
miles to as much as 1200
square miles, although
fenced boundaries and
habitat destruction restrict
them to much smaller areas
in most parts of the country.

Above: It may not look elegant . . . but itches have to be satisfied!

must act as the focal point of their communal activity.

Both Asian and African elephants conform to the same codes of social behavior, that is, they both live in herds of individuals who are in all probability related to each other genetically. The main unit, numbering from 10 to 50 animals, consists of overlapping generations, spanning anything up to 60 or 70 years. Occasionally, vast gatherings of hundreds of elephants are reported, but these are temporary and are almost certainly brought about by food and/or water availability at critical times of the year. As conditions change, the large crowd breaks up into its former units – although some rearranging of individuals will undoubtedly have taken place – which move away from each other to reoccupy their former areas.

Even under normal conditions of food and water abundance, the small family unit may roam in an area containing other such units to which it is related. Thus, family units may form only part of larger kinship units whose members will frequently meet and spend time together before separating once more. Within each of these units, and therefore within the whole kinship unit, the predominant animals are variously-aged females and calves. To these females falls the sole responsibility of rearing the young. They are devoted to their offspring for some years. To cross the

path of such an elephant is to court a defensive reaction that is unparalleled in the animal kingdom. The calves are born infrequently, take years to mature and in each of them, as in a human infant, is invested not only a great deal of time and energy but also the reproductive future of the unit.

Before the arrival of the young elephant into the world, its coming birth is known to the whole herd of females and young. For them, the birth of a calf is something of an occasion. The female who is nearing the end of a pregnancy that has lasted for almost two years (the gestation period is 20–22 months) becomes the focus of attention as her closest relatives protect her from possible danger and attend the moment of delivery. For years afterward, this attention will not be slackened, for it is during its early infancy that the calf will be at its most vulnerable to predators – particularly in Southeast Asia where tigers reportedly once accounted for as many as one quarter of all newborn elephants (a figure that must now be decreasing, given the fact that human activity has almost succeeded in exterminating the tiger).

If the responsibilities of care of the young have fallen so heavily upon the females' shoulders, one might legitimately inquire what role the males perform. The father of the new calf may actually be miles away, having very likely played his part in siring other youngsters to be born into family

Left: Where the danger from predators is high, elephant herds tend to become larger, numbering over 100 animals. If food is in short supply, however, the groups become much smaller.

units elsewhere. It is doubtful whether he would recognize his own offspring if he met them. His role is forced upon him for sound evolutionary reasons. If we follow the development of the new-born calf within the female dominated family unit it becomes easy to see that until a certain age has been reached the sex of the infant is of no concern to the adults around it. Its survival is all that matters. Once this has been guaranteed and the maturing elephant begins to show more obviously the characteristics of being either male or female, the herd adopts a different attitude toward it. There would be no natural advantage gained by brother and sister elephants interbreeding. One of them must go. The females must stay behind to learn about child care while the males are forcibly sent out to wander the bush in teenage groups in search of willing females to whom they are not closely related and with whom they will form only temporary but surprisingly affectionate relationships.

At birth, the calf already weighs more than the average man. When it takes its first steps – within a few minutes – it measures some three feet in height, just big enough to suckle from its mother's breasts. These breasts differ from those of most other mammals in that they are reduced in number to only one pair – as in humans. They are situated just behind the front legs. Contrary to popular belief the calf does not use its trunk to

suckle milk. It rolls it back over its own head to expose its fleshy mouth. This it clamps onto the nipple where it is able to effect the strong mechanical and rhythmic sucking action required to draw the milk through the nipple and into its mouth.

Throughout these first tentative explorations, the calf and its mother are closely guarded by the other females. It will take at least 48 hours before the youngster is sufficiently strong to follow even a slowly moving herd. In Africa, lions form one of the greatest dangers to such a vulnerable young elephant. So the calf stays close to its mother's side, held by its need for both her milk and her physical protection. Should it stray too far, she will use her trunk to guide it back to its refuge under her belly and between her legs. Occasionally, another female will 'adopt' the youngster on a temporary basis, and if she is herself producing milk she will suckle the calf as though it were her own.

Within its first year the calf should be starting to nourish itself with vegetation. However, many calves continue to suckle for two or three years after this, depending on the mother's attitude, her supply of milk, and the arrival of the next calf. The first thing that a youngster will do when its immediate ties to a mature female are released will be to associate more closely with the other calves of the family unit. Its mother remains watchful of

As elephants giving birth in the wild vehemently defend their privacy, it is often only in zoos that newborn elephants may be seen and photographed. The baby weighs about 180–240lb and stands about 3 feet high at the shoulder. Its first vital task is to find its mother's nipples (one can be seen at top left in the picture, right) and suckle milk — with its mouth, not with its trunk.

its movements and is ever present to help a young elephant to scramble up a steep bank or over a fallen tree. Other females – with or without their own young – are equally attentive and willing to show guidance when new situations are encountered. The adult trunk is also a useful tool for administering punishment when the eager youngster does something foolishly dangerous or oversteps the mark in playfulness with its more sober seniors.

So, by degrees, the youngster is integrated into the family unit as it moves from the close protection of the adult females to the playful group of other juniors. It remains in this mixed age group of elephants, which will occasionally be visited by bulls whose intentions are purely sexual. There is usually a group of these bulls – themselves headed by a senior animal – in the vicinity of the cows, although when their masculine attentions are not focused on sex, they may lag a mile or so behind. As a result, these bulls play no part in the task of keeping the playful young in order.

When a waterhole is visited, the smaller calves will immediately leap in and splash around, sending showers of water over their more stately elders who want only to cool and water themselves in peace. The older cows are quick to take advantage of their youngsters' muddy preoccupations and will retire to a shaded feeding spot while younger cows gain experience in child care

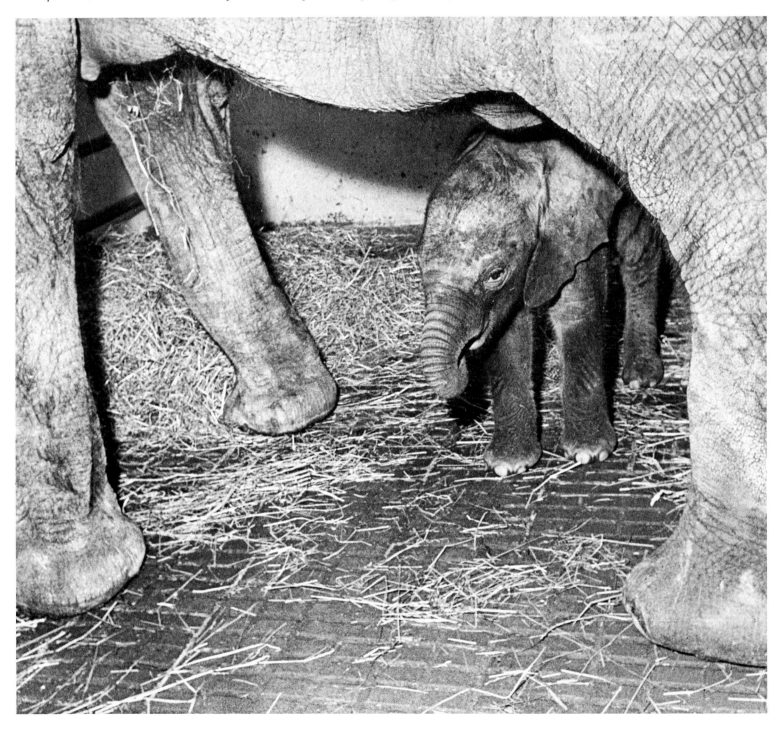

The first days of a life

'The breasts of a young African elephant, pregnant for the first time, swell up from her flat chest in preparation for lactation, but older cows may lactate from one birth to the next and the size of their breasts cannot be used as a clue. I never actually witnessed the moment of birth although I came close to it on three occasions. As such observations are rare, I have drawn fairly fully from my field notes to describe the first hours of life.

The first time was when I encountered the family of the matriarch Deino in a clearing in the South Endabash Scrub. She was a fairly wild elephant and needed to be approached with caution to avoid scaring her. One of this group, a young female of fourteen years, had just given birth. Under her belly stood a very small calf which was still smeared in wet blood. Blood also covered the mother's hind legs and trunk, and was daubed on the trunks of two large females of this group, suggesting that they might have picked up the afterbirth or somehow assisted in the delivery. The calf was red brown and hairy. Its membranous ears fitted perfectly like leaves around the heart of a cabbage. Its body was thin and crumpled compared to the bulging stomachs of older calves. The mother stood exhausted, unwilling to move, but the older cows began to shake their heads and trumpet. Knowing their nervous behaviour, I did not wish to disturb them further lest the calf should come to harm, so, after a few minutes, I left.

Another time I was able to get much closer to a young cow named Tusked Ear who had just given birth. She was one of those juveniles that become pregnant at an early age; she must have been still under thirteen years. At some stage in her life her left ear had been severely ripped by a bad-tempered elder. Her matriarch, a one-tusker named Aphrodite, lived in the Ground Water Forest near the Park entrance gate, and seldom came out of it. They were not driven to seek cover because of a nervous disposition, but they seemed to restrict themselves voluntarily to this small but rich segment of the Park. Part of their range included either side of the escarpment road going from the village up to the hotel, on the way to Ngorongoro, and it was here on the Park Boundaries that Tusked Ear bore a male calf at about midday.

I happened to be passing just at this time and saw the bloody afterbirth freshly deposited in the middle of the road with a cluster of six elephants on the verge standing around a tiny calf. He was smaller than average for a new-born, which is often the case when the mother is still a growing adolescent (genetic factors presumably being modified by the internal environment). The matriarch was a little way off browsing as if nothing had happened that concerned her. Within the group around the baby were a full grown cow, Electra, her two calves of five-and-a-half and a year, a nine-year-old female and Tusked Ear herself. The young mother looked exhausted. Her head dropped and her legs sagged as if she could hardly stand. She had no energy left for her baby and seemed withdrawn and somnolent. The only attention he received was from the nine-year-old female who let her trunk wander over his face fondling every smallest part.

The calf tried to suck with its mouth, unsuccessfully, once or twice from his mother and then tottered over to the large cow Electra. What followed amazed me. Electra paid absolutely no attention until he was right under her stomach and then suddenly kicked him with a hind leg three times, sending him sprawling. The new-born calf bowled over in the dust, picked himself up and staggered back towards his mother.

The nine-year-old, who had been following his movements intently, opened her forelegs and pulling the baby under her belly, straddled him protectively. This action moved Tusked Ear enough for her to extend her trunk weakly and touch the baby on his forehead. He swayed gently under the female calf for a few minutes and then tried once again to approach Electra. He was sent flying with another kick. The female calf stood over him and rubbed his back.

Several cars passed by, or stopped so that the tourists packed inside could take pictures, and chat and shout to each other.

A noisy tipper truck clattered down the road showering the elephants with dust and alarming the female calf so that she pushed the new-born male to his feet with her forefoot.... They were used to cars here. Electra's one-year-old was allowed to suck from her, and the rejected new-born tried to suck from his protective nine-year-old friend. Shortly afterwards Electra began to move off downhill, summoned by a rumble from Aphrodite. The female calf started to follow but the new-born who went with her collapsed after a few paces and she would not leave him. Tusked Ear growled and Electra turned round and came back. Painfully slowly they made their way down the steep rocky hill, with the new-born calf collapsing every few paces and the whole group standing for long periods before moving on.

When I saw this calf again after several weeks he was thriving well, and had filled out, losing his crumpled bag appearance, but since his matriarch chose to live in the sheltering forest and seldom came out, I could not follow his progress in detail.'

and stand guard over the adolescents.

When the family unit is on the move, its members usually travel in single file along well-defined elephant trails. Such trails may have been used for hundreds of years by successive generations and one of the main problems for humans is how to divert these determined quadrupeds from a route once trodden by their ancestors. At the first scent of danger the strung-out formation is immediately abandoned as calves cluster together and are surrounded by the females who search the air with their trunks to locate the source of their collective agitation. Once detected, the enemy is faced and the senior cow – the matriarch – will advance a few paces, signalling her annoyance with outstretched ears, pointing trunk, and dust-stirring feet. Other females may advance with her, ready to defend at all costs. If the bulls are in the immediate vicinity, they will respond to any trumpetings of alarm and make their way toward the scene of the disturbance.

For humans in game parks, this situation can offer one of the greatest dangers: to be caught between groups of agitated elephants as they

A baby elephant tentatively seeks the foliage among the long, sharp spines of an acacia bush. Although it may start pulling at leaves and grasses while only a few months old, it will not be weaned completely for several years.

Above: Elephants in Africa migrate considerable distances for reasons which are not fully understood. Water, weather, and the amount of food available are influential factors; but the seasons of food plants, and parasites, may also play a part.

converge on a common enemy – perhaps a vehicle containing tourists caught up in the excitement of photographing elephants on the move. I once stopped in a Kenyan game park to photograph a baby elephant standing some 30 yards to the right of the track. Behind it – and also to the right – were several large females browsing lazily among the overhanging branches of acacia trees. The peacefulness of the heat-hazed scene was rudely disrupted by an elderly, well-tusked female – perhaps the calf's mother or even the matriarch – who broke cover on the left and charged straight at my Land Rover. Her ears were outstretched, her trunk was curled back behind her hefty tusks and her legs were splayed in the characteristic soles-forward manner of an elephant in full flight. She screamed with rage, intensified perhaps by the realization of her own slackness at being so easily separated from the youngster. She was obviously in no mood to be opposed. To have remained on the track in the hope that she was merely bluffing would have been to court certain disaster. I pulled away at high speed when she was no more than 20 paces away and, with a hasty glance in the rear mirror, I saw her looming out of the dust, still charging. She did not give up until she was a good 70 yards away from the calf. About 100 yards back, I saw three very large males making their way straight toward the scene. Their trunks were

held forward, testing the air. They were probably responding to the female's screams. I felt relieved that they had not been browsing any closer, let alone approaching along my only escape route.

It is only by piecing together such experiences that one is able to begin to understand the real nature of community life among elephants. An apparently isolated band of elephants should warn the observer that others may be in the vicinity. The young themselves are not at all dangerous, but they signal the close proximity of adults. With a bit of knowledge of their ways, they can be watched and photographed for hours at a time. Ignorance spells trouble, as two examples show. A man in Zaire – when it was the Belgian Congo – once approached a lone male elephant on foot in order to get good photographs of it; and in another incident a Kenyan tourist stepped out of his car to offer an elephant a bun! Both lost their lives.

The calf's survival depends upon a certain appreciation of the world around it. The calf's natural curiosity for exploring and testing its surroundings must be carefully held in check by the more experienced and knowledgeable elephants around it. The bond between mother and offspring is consequently a very strong one, to the extent that some females – especially those who have given birth only once – may be overconcerned for the welfare of their young. A more placid approach to childcare is generally exhibited by the mature and experienced females. There was one elephant in Uganda whose relationship with her child was so strong that even after the premature death of her infant she managed to carry the decaying corpse around with her for several days before finally abandoning it. Another striking example of maternal instinct comes from Lieutenant Colonel J H Williams, who spent the postwar years of his life working with Asian elephants in Burma. His book *Elephant Bill* contains an account of an action which he describes as one of the most intelligent he has ever witnessed an elephant perform. It is also an act of true courage and one of a love between mother and child that might mistakenly be considered the sole prerogative of human beings. It is an episode worth quoting at length (see box on pages 76–77).

Whatever biologists may tell us of the benefits gained by an individual animal who abandons its offspring at times so that it can survive itself, in order to breed many more times, there can be no doubt that Ma Shwe was so devoted to her daughter that she really was prepared to risk her own life. When one stops to think how much time and energy is devoted by females to their young, it is perhaps not surprising to see that they will go to such extraordinary lengths to keep them alive.

That kind of devotion is a common feature of

Below: An elephant herd on the move usually travels in single file, along trails which have been used by previous generations of elephants.

Above: It looks as if it is laughing; but with tail cocked and head held high, this young elephant is alarmed, though not bold enough to attack.

female elephants until such a time – about six months – that the youngsters begin to stray from their sides. Away from its mother the maturing calf cannot command the immediate attention usual in its former months. Indeed, the mother may enjoy the relaxation of her duties to such an extent that the little calf is sometimes in danger of being left behind when the family unit moves on to fresh feeding grounds. Usually, however, one or more of the younger females will be keeping a wary eye open for juvenile stragglers. Sylvia Sikes once noted a panic-striken herd of elephants – a large-tusked visiting bull had been shot – leave a six-month-old calf stranded in a steep sided valley.

A seven- or eight-year-old female, too young to have given birth, turned and helped the calf to clamber up the steep slope. Her plight was noticed by a slightly older brother who turned to assist the struggling duo. While the female protected the calf, the young bull picked out the easiest route for them all to follow up the side of the valley.

It is interesting to reflect that this situation may represent the opposite to the behavior of Ma Shwe in the raging river. Perhaps the mother of this calf was fully aware of the danger to herself in retrieving her youngster, and perhaps she had abandoned it in the presence of gun-bearing humans in order that she might herself survive.

Above: In its first months a baby elephant gambols in high spirits. Its mother or its elder sibling will fetch it if it wanders too far.

Above: A baby elephant stops its mother for a drink. With about 21 percent fat content, elephant's milk is similar to cow's milk.

Ma Shwe: a mother's love

'One evening, when the Upper Taungdwin River was in a heavy spate, I was listening and hoping to hear the boom and roar of timber coming from upstream. Directly below my camp the banks of the river were steep and rocky and twelve to fifteen feet high. About fifty yards away on the other side, the bank was made up of ledges of shale strata. Although it was already nearly dusk, by watching these ledges being successfully submerged, I was trying to judge how fast the water was rising.

I was suddenly alarmed by hearing an elephant roaring as though frightened, and, looking down, I saw three or four men rushing up and down on the opposite bank in a state of great excitement. I realised at once that something was wrong, and ran down to the edge of the near bank and there saw Ma Shwe (Miss Gold) with her three-months-old-calf, trapped in the fast-rising torrent. She herself was still in her depth, as the water was about six feet deep. But there was a life-and-death struggle going on. Her calf was screaming with terror and was afloat like a cork. Ma Shwe was as near to the far bank as she could get, holding her whole body against the raging and increasing torrent, and keeping the calf pressed against her massive body. Every now and then the swirling water would sweep the calf away; then, with terrific strength, she would encircle it

be able to place it on a narrow shelf of rock, five feet above the flood level. Having accomplished this, she fell back into the raging torrent, and she herself went away like a cork. She well knew that she would now have a fight to save her own life, as, less than three hundred yards below where she had stowed her calf in safety, there was a gorge. If she were carried down, it would be certain death. I knew, as well as she did, that there was one spot between her and the gorge where she could get up the bank, but it was on the other side from where she had put her calf. By that time my chief interest was in the calf. It stood, tucked up, shivering and terrified on a ledge just wide enough to hold its feet. Its little, fat, protruding belly was tightly pressed against the bank.

While I was peering over at it from about eight feet above, wondering what I could do next, I heard the grandest sounds of a mother's love I can remember. Ma Shwe had crossed the river and got up the bank, and was making her way back as fast as she could, calling the whole time – a defiant roar, but to her calf it was music. The two little ears, like maps of India, were cocked forward, listening to the only sound that mattered, the call of her mother.

Any wild schemes which had raced through my head of recovering the calf by ropes disappeared as fast as I had formed them, when I saw Ma Shwe emerge from the jungle and appear on the opposite bank. When she saw her calf, she stopped roaring and began rumbling, a never-to-be-forgotten sound, not unlike that made by a very high-powered car when accelerating. It is the sound of pleasure, like a cat's purring, and delighted she must have been to see her calf still in the same spot, where she had put her half an hour before.

As darkness fell, the muffled boom of floating logs hitting against each other came from upstream. A torrential rain was falling, and the river still separated the mother and her calf. I decided that I could do nothing but wait and see what happened. Twice before turning in for the night I went down to the bank and picked out the calf with my torch, but this seemed to disturb it, so I went away.

It was just as well I did, because at dawn Ma Shwe and her calf were together – both on the far bank. The spate had subsided to a mere foot of dirty-coloured water. No one in the camp had seen Ma Shwe recover her calf, but she must have lifted it down from the ledge in the same way as she had put it there. Five years later, when the calf came to be named, the Burmans christened it Ma Yay Yee (Miss Laughing Water).'

An extract from Elephant Bill

with her trunk and pull it upstream to rest against her body again.

There was a sudden rise in the water, as if a two-foot bore had come down, and the calf was washed clean over the mother's hindquarters and was gone. She turned to chase it, like an otter after a fish, but she had travelled about fifty yards downstream and, plunging and sometimes afloat, had crossed to my side of the river, before she had caught up with it and got it back. For what seemed minutes, she pinned the calf with her head and trunk against the rocky bank. Then, with a really gigantic effort, she picked it up in her trunk and reared up until she was half standing on her hind legs, so as to

Right: Not only does the
mother elephant guard her
baby closely – the whole
herd is usually very
protective and gentle
toward its youngest
members.

Could it also be that the male and female who risked their lives to assist the calf were actually protecting the older female – in her reproductive prime – from possible death? The two elephants who had helped the calf were not of a reproductive age, and they were possibly more expendable than an older female of proven fertility. Perhaps, again, the incident merely reflects the flexibility in the relationships that link groups as the calf begins to mature.

Between one and two years old, the young elephant has well and truly embarked upon the long trail of learning. Its first preoccupation, once it has less access to a supply of milk, is to feed for itself. At what stage the calf begins to rely on the vegetation it can collect on its own is still something of a mystery because of the length of time that so many calves continue to suckle milk. But its inquisitive trunk will have given it ample opportunity to practice picking leaves from bushes and grass from the ground. While close to its mother's side it will have played with such food items dropped from her mouth and may even have tested them for itself. Grasses make up the bulk of the diet, although a great many different types of vegetation are readily consumed according to their availability and the season of the year. When the calf is older it will find the bark of certain trees a delicacy, especially during the dry months when ground vegetation is nutritionally poor.

Calves of about a year and more engage in trials of strength and tests of each other's characters and moods. It is important that these individual attributes are known by all those with whom many years of adult life are to be shared. The young males seem to be the most vigorous in these contests and indeed it is this trait which, 10 years later, eventually leads the matriarch to take the firm but necessary steps to expel them from the company of their close relatives.

At this stage, however, their exuberance is tolerated because they still have much to learn about survival. Their prepubescent sisters will be busy helping with any new arrivals to the unit and generally easing the maternal burden of the older females. Much of the learning of all the young, regardless of their age, is done by watching and imitating. It is quite usual to see them tearing small branches from overhanging trees and then discarding them, the object being more to gain useful food-gathering experience than to satisfy any immediate pangs of hunger.

When water is scarce adults will move toward a sandy riverbed and dig a hole with their feet and tusks. Then they stand and wait for it to fill slowly with water seeping through from a low level. The young watch and often paw eagerly at the surrounding sand themselves, though they usually end up dipping their trunks into the more expert excavations nearby. Significantly, when

Left: The affection shown by a mother elephant to her calf does not cease when she gives birth to another. Often a family unit of two or three siblings is created, the calves playing together and older ones looking after the baby.

water is really scarce and the family units are besieged by prolonged droughts, the adults are less likely to tolerate youngsters barging in for a free drink after a really deep hole has been laboriously dug and only a small amount of water has slowly trickled into it. Each elephant needs several gallons of water a day and when their survival is suddenly at stake the adults, the least expendable members of the unit, are less favorably disposed toward the young. When water is plentiful the splashing calves find ample opportunity to get used to water. Both Asian and African elephants are good swimmers and both help their calves across fast-flowing rivers by swimming downstream of them, so that the force of the current keeps the youngster pressed against its mother's side.

The elephant may seem one of the more unlikely land creatures to be good at swimming, but in fact it takes to the water willingly and expertly. One Asian elephant once went on a grand tour of the islands of the Bay of Bengal. Apparently it thought little of swimming more than a mile between some of the islands and its total journey of about 200 miles took it the best part of 12 years to complete. African elephants have been recorded well out of their depth in such famous waterways as the Nile and the Zambezi. Quite small calves have been seen to accompany adults on these journeys, having gained the confidence to tackle such daunting obstacles from their playful antics in the waterholes and streams of the surrounding bush.

There is obviously great long-term value in calves being allowed to explore for themselves within the boundaries of safety. The young take a long time to mature, and are able to learn a great deal from adults which increases their chances of survival in later life.

The onset of sexual maturity is the change that relinquishes them from the feminine care that has been lavished upon them for so many years. The strong ties between the individuals remain, of course, but there is a new generation of elephants growing up and it is on these inexperienced and vulnerable calves that the unit must focus attention.

Our former juveniles are now adolescents taking their places in the structure of elephant society. The female, her maternal instincts with the unit still developing, now awaits her first relationship with a visiting male, and her first pregnancy. She will teach her first calf all the rules that brought her so successfully through her first dozen or so years.

Life is not quite so straightforward for the developing male. His restless antics of the past few years culminate in his making sexual advances toward the females of his own family unit. Now is the time for him to go in pursuit elsewhere. The

In general elephants coexist amicably with the other wild animals that share their domain. There is some evidence, however, that they do not tolerate black rhinos, and the alarm shown by the elephant (above) may be due to this antagonism. Often young elephants will playfully chase or tease bush pigs, although those at left are so busy fighting that they have not even noticed their inquisitive companion.

Bottom: Using its tusks as picks and its trunk as a shovel, an elephant excavates a hole by the river, possibly in search of salt which all elephants love.

Below: Indian elephants swim just as well as African elephants, using their trunks as snorkels to breathe through.

Above: An elephant keeps cool by blowing a fine spray of water over itself, especially over its ears where evaporation cools the blood.

Above: Two piapiacs (a type of crow) perched on an elephant gain a fine view of insects and other food kicked up by the elephant as it walks.

Left: Young bulls spar to define their position in the herd hierarchy. Dominance is usually established by size and threat display; violence is rare among bulls, even in the presence of a female in season.

matriarch – who may be his mother – is increasingly agitated by his disruptive presence within the unit. She interrupts his advances and forces him to the fringes of society. When he tries to return she pushes him out again and again, taking little heed either of his reluctance to be separated from his close relatives or of her own strong ties with him. Her responsibility lies with the unit and she will welcome only the advances of males who are not too closely related with the females around her. Incest is as much a taboo among elephants, apparently, as it is among humans. Inbreeding is not generally successful in evolutionary terms and her behavior is genetically controlled to prevent it from happening.

The young male soon realizes that his presence within the unit will be tolerated no longer and that to avoid being attacked he must keep his distance. The contented larynx-rumblings of the females keep him informed of their position in the bush or jungle and he will follow them around, taking care not to be seen to be too close. It must be a difficult time for the youngster, not yet established as a mature individual and yet banished from the sides of the elephants with whom he has shared every moment of the last dozen years of life. Eventually he meets similarly placed bulls from whose company he is not excluded. They can now engage in their trials of strength without being castigated and as more of them

meet up and wrestle playfully they form a loose hierarchy of dominance.

These bull herds – which on rare occasions may number more than 100 individuals – are naturally comprised of elephants of different ages, from those freshly emancipated to the grand old sire bulls of advanced years. Their biological function is simply reproductive and when a group of 10 or so meets up with a unit of females, their preceding trials of strength and the consequent respect for the differences between them will already have established who has immediate access to the cows and who must wait his turn. The largest bulls are the oldest and it is to them that the privilege falls. The matriarch is fully aware of their presence and she knows instinctively that when she or one of her cows is on heat, the close proximity of the males must be tolerated. However what follows is not quite what one might expect from these brief encounters.

Throughout their bachelor wanderings the bulls harbor deep respect and affection for their females that is equalled by few animals in the world today. Obviously, the close ties of their youth are never really broken. Once they are given the rare opportunity to resume contact with the opposite sex they indulge in a reunion of courtship, love, and sex that is atypical of partners who spend so short a time together.

The males begin to form a loose association

Above: Male and female elephants often demonstrate affection with gentle caresses.

Above: Few animals can provide an example of a closer family unit than the elephant.

with the female unit some time before any of the cows comes on heat. The matriarch is usually aware of the significance of their movements and she is largely tolerant of their awakening interests. It is, after all, in her interest to have a strong male escort in the vicinity in case any danger requiring a show of strength and ivory should arise.

Day by day the two groups come closer together until a privileged bull begins to show a special interest in a particular cow as she browses at the edge of her unit. The two may be seen together with increasing frequency, getting to know each other and testing each other's moods and emotions. For a few moments, every now and then, they cautiously investigate each other with their trunks, rough hide scrapes against hide and two great bony heads press occasionally against each other. If there was ever any doubt that the two would see their growing intimacy through to the end, it is dramatically dispelled from the moment the cow comes on heat. Suddenly her mild responses become more urgent as the effect of hormones which previously circulated in her blood at only low levels, is felt. Now she goads her male into action, looking for the right approach that will spur him into sexual action rather than convince him that once again he is to be banished by a member of the opposite sex. She touches him with her trunk, then retreats and advances once more. Trumpeting excitement, he attempts to mount her from behind, but she slides from under him and moves away. He hesitates, again perhaps reminded of his youthful rejection, but she turns and signals her approval by flapping her ears and coiling her trunk. He approaches and she stands still as he mounts her once more. This time she does not move away and as he positions himself, forelegs lying along her back, his penis penetrates her. The union is short, perhaps a minute or two, until the transfer of genetic material is completed. Expended, he dismounts and moves away a short distance to feed. Her excitement soon dies and she is quick to join him.

Already their association, so intense and short, is on the ebb. They browse together and may even copulate again. However, for the male, the task is done and he now becomes increasingly aware of the feminine will to see him removed to a respectable distance. It is true that some couples remain closely associated for weeks or even months, but the pressure on him to go must be present from the moment that copulation takes place.

The cows take care of the pregnant female for the next 22 months and she will not conceive again for at least a year after that. Her days will be spent with the other females, each producing a calf every three or four years throughout their lives. The young females will remain, the young males will be banished once again to the bush.

Above: A young female elephant, probably in estrus for the first time, is startled by the pursuit of an excited and much larger bull.

The dominance of the bull over the other males of the herd is asserted as he mates with the female. The actual mating is brief, lasting less than a minute, but it may be repeated two or three times at intervals of a few hours. No pair-bond is formed, and the elephants soon resume their usual life in the herd.

4:SERVANT AND GOD

The average weight of a man from Southeast Asia is about 140lb. That of a bull elephant from the same region is about 13,440lb, nearly 100 times as much. On a purely physical basis, it is difficult to see how such a disparity could have allowed the elephant to be so easily subdued and led to the workhouse, there to spend the prime of its life obeying the orders of its diminutive captor. Yet that has been the situation in India, Ceylon, Burma, and other parts of Southeast Asia for centuries.

When early humans first took to hunting in organized groups in Southeast Asia, perhaps over a million years ago, the elephant was already a well-established animal of the forest. As a prey supplying vast quantities of meat, it must have commanded the special attentions of the human hunter. In addition the ribs could be fashioned into arrows and spearheads, the vast hides could be used to keep out the cold of night or spread wide across the floor of a damp cave, and the tusks were easy to carve into weapons and domestic implements. Without doubt, an elephant must have been a prize indeed.

The predator-prey relationship must have remained unchanged for thousands of years, until the development of large-scale cultivation of crops. This revolution brought a more sedentary way of life for humans about 10,000 years ago. Villages developed and large labor forces were established to fell and collect trees from nearby forests. Wood, one of the more important ingredients of the lives of our ancestors, was abundant and used not only for building houses, fences, and tools but also for fuelling fires with which to cook and keep out both cold and wild animals.

Imagine, then, this sequence of events, perhaps repeated with variations countless times in hundreds of scattered communities: an elephant mother is killed and the orphaned calf is adopted by one of the more sympathetic hunters. The young elephant, inquisitive once familiarized with its new surroundings, and fed by the women of the village, soon begins exploring its new home and testing the objects around it. One day, a woman is struggling with her load. She pauses for a rest and the calf she has often fed recognizes her and comes forward. It playfully wraps its trunk around her heavy goods and wanders off with its trophy. The woman is quick to grasp the significance of the incident. Here is a placid young animal of immense strength, but tame, and quite able to perform tasks beyond human strength.

Once the elephant's willingness to co-operate was established – in return for ample food and rest – man's tasks in the great forests of Southeast Asia could be eased. Here, at last, was a means of transporting heavy logs from the site of their felling to distant camps and to rivers, where the current would send them on their way downstream to be collected and used by other communities. This latter scheme must have encouraged men to establish villages along riverways which were far from the forests and near the coastline.

Because detailed records of human behavior did not begin until just a few thousand years ago, there is no way of knowing exactly what the relationship between man and the Asian elephant was until comparatively recently – that is, during the last four or five thousand years. Both archeological and literary sources indicate that the relationship between the two was strong; it was among the first significant interactions between man and his environment to be immortalized in literature. Such ancient documents as *Gaja Sastre* and the *Rig Veda* from 2000 BC describe in amazing detail not only elephant life and habits but, they also show a distribution taking in such areas as Iran, Baluchistan, the Hindu Kush, and the length of the River Ganges.

In such areas today, the Asian elephant is virtually extinct, for this elephant suddenly harnessed by man the agriculturalist, contributed to its own demise. Domesticated elephants speeded the process of forest clearance and as the trees made way for crops, the wild elephants were increasingly denied places in which to live. Within the last thousand years or so, the elephant has been forced eastward from Central Asia not only as a result of habitat destruction but also from the increase in trapping and the advent of large-scale ivory hunting. The use of the elephant as a war vehicle led to the wholesale capture and slaughter of thousands more of them.

Like many animals today, the elephant survives only in those places which have so far proved inaccessible to humans. Such areas are diminishing. Since India gained its independence in 1947 there has been a very great movement toward clearing the remaining forests to open up new agricultural land. Thus, to survive, wild elephants must keep moving to new areas, even those at great altitudes where their ancestors would never have been found. The most up to date figures show that there may be no more than from 28,000 – 42,000 wild Asian elephants in existence today.

There are obviously many problems encountered when attempts are made to compile statistics of this nature. Nevertheless, when compared to the countless thousands of elephants that once existed across a vast and continuous portion of the eastern world, Robert Olivier's final comment in his seminal 1978 paper is particularly poignant. He says, 'In view of these small numbers and the continuing exponential escalation of the human activities responsible for them, as well as certain relevant characteristics of large, long-lived animals, the Asian elephant is now officially considered an endangered species.'

Above: One of Asia's ageless scenes: at a quiet command from its mahout, an elephant pushes over a tree in the Sri Lankan forest.

Right: Between a good mahout and his elephant, an intimate relationship of obedience, trust, and affection is built to last a lifetime.

Ironically, while the wild Asian elephant has been pushed toward a seemingly inevitable extinction, its domesticated counterpart has been raised to an exalted position within Southeast Asian society. When there are no elephants left in the wild, the image of the elephant as man's servant and god, an image that has been with us for many centuries, will survive, but not for long. When there are no free-ranging breeding stocks available, the days of the domesticated elephant will be numbered. It will mean the end of a relationship that has been one of the hallmarks of human society in that region of the world, in commerce, warfare, and religion.

When man first used the elephant to bulldoze through the expansive forests and then to haul great logs through miles of undergrowth, it could not have taken him long to realize that to breed his work animals in captivity was a highly un-economical state of affairs. If a pregnant cow was captured, she could do no work during the last

months of her pregnancy and would then need to spend two or even three years in close association with her calf. After that time she could work sporadically but her offspring would still need some of her attention as it grew toward its independence. It would not actually be of a trainable age itself until it was well into its tenth year of life. Throughout this period both animals would have to be fed, watered, and housed. Clearly, it was more efficient for man to go out and catch his elephants at an age when they were strong, trainable, and able to be put to work almost immediately.

The capture of individual elephants must have posed something of a problem, at least at first when there were no captive ones to assist in the hunt. When killing for food it would have been comparatively easy to track down a herd, single out a victim, and then to move in and aim several spears at it, hoping that it would be injured enough to lag behind its companions where it could be more easily dispatched.

Capture would have been more problematical. By carefully following the animals, humans would have soon learned that elephants use regular tracks through the forest and that, although they can feed almost anywhere, their need for large quantities of water forces them – during dry periods at least – to make predictable journeys along chosen routes.

A number of techniques for capturing elephants suggest themselves, all with grave disadvantages. By digging specially shaped holes in the ground – just long enough and deep enough, and tapering toward the bottom to pin the elephant's legs together – men could catch some animals. However elephants trapped in this way often sustained injury and were of little use afterward except as food. Also an individual that stepped onto the carefully concealed surface of the pitfall trap would not necessarily be of an ideal age for training.

Lassoing may have been another technique employed and it would have had the advantage of allowing the right animals to be selected in advance. Twisted vines strategically placed on the ground or at head height could be loosely knotted and then pulled tight at the required moment. Successfully captured individuals would be tied to a tree and left to calm down before being led away to their new life. However, there would have been

the risk of injuring an elephant's trunk. Where a foot was to be snared, only the back foot could be caught – a trapped front foot would cause an elephant to lose its balance and fall, with the risk of damaging itself.

The business of capturing and training elephants for their major role, as workers in lumber operations, has been practiced for hundreds of years in Asia.

The method of capture, that of driving the animals toward a *keddah* or stockade must have been handed down through thousands of years and the modern techniques, in use well into this century, must have been very similar to that used during previous centuries. The principle of the *keddah* operation was very simple, though large in scale. An area of jungle containing a source of water known to be frequented by elephants was fenced off and the elephants driven into the pen through a special opening which was sealed behind them. To put such an operation into practice and bring it to a successful conclusion could take months, requiring the co-operation of thousands of men from villages throughout a large expanse of forest.

Their initial task was to locate a watering place where herds of elephants were bound to congregate during the dry periods of the year. At a time when the elephants were elsewhere, the men set to work building a strong wooden fence

Left: Domesticated elephants in India may be so gentle that they are entrusted with the care of small children.

Above: Sunlight, shafting into dense bamboo jungle in India, highlights a peaceful group of wild elephants.

around the whole area of forest containing the water. The overall shape of the fence varied but a triangular one was commonly adopted with the two sides running from the apex to the base extended to form a gigantic letter 'A.' The crossbar of the 'A' contained an opening, the *kan gula* or 'ear hole,' which could be closed quickly with a lightweight wooden barrier that unrolled from above when released from its roped position. When the scene was set, the villagers waited patiently until water was scarce and the elephants were beginning to congregate around their chosen places to drink and bathe. Many of these areas would have been blocked off previously so the elephants had to keep moving from one site to the next, gradually coming within range of the villagers.

When the time was right, thousands of men fanned out across the countryside to form a huge wall around the elephants. They were often many miles from the stockade, but once into position they moved slowly but surely toward their destination. The great thing was not to alarm the elephants to the extent that they panicked and broke back through the advancing lines. Progress was inevitably slow, but day by day the enclosed elephants moved closer to the water in the stockade. The men formed a huge square virtually around the unsuspecting elephants and when the base of the A-shaped *keddah* was finally reached, the line of men nearest it broke away leaving a clear run to the inner trap with its attractive source of water. The surrounding beaters then began to move in, increasing their volume of noise just enough to distract the elephants from the implications of the 'ear hole' opening ahead of them. Usually the promise of the water, which was by now tantalizingly close, was enough to lure them through. When they had all passed safely through and into the forested stockade, the ropes were cut and the barrier fell into place. There must have been much celebrating among the men whose patient weeks of jungle stalking were at an end.

For others, the task of actually moving into the stockade and picking out those elephants suitable for training could now begin. For this purpose, elephants which had already been trained were used. These elephants, bearing their mahout riders, with another man armed with ropes seated behind, entered the stockade when the wild elephants were watered and at rest. They tackled the dangerous mission of roping the captured animals to trees strong enough to hold them. By this time the wild elephants would have become suspicious of their new surroundings, encircled as they were by hordes of human beings, and groups of them would be moving about in an agitated manner.

The sight of the domesticated animals moving quietly among them generally had something of a

Above: Even elephants born in captivity cannot begin training until about 10 years old.

Above: Lassoes made from twisted vines are a traditional method of elephant capture.

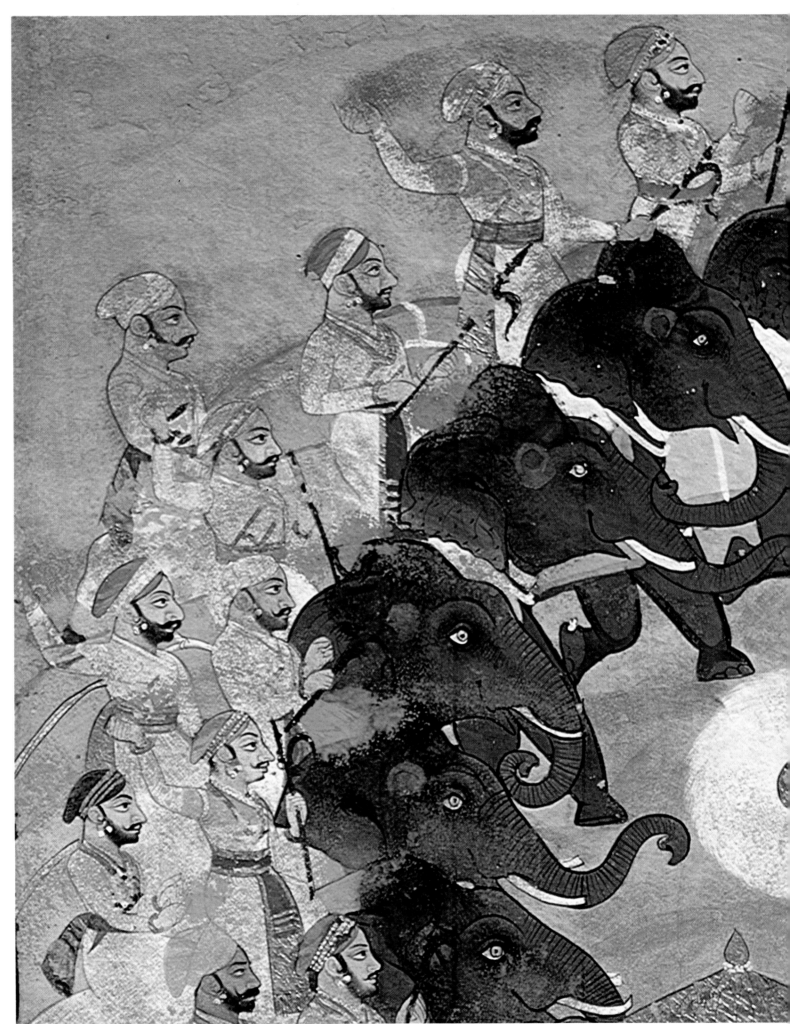

Above: A maharajah (with black-feathered banner) and his elephant-mounted troops throw colored powder to celebrate Krishna's festival.

Right: At the start of the
elephant drive, beaters
gather in the jungle before
dispersing to encircle the
wild elephant herds.

Opposite: Tame elephants
and their mahouts (above)
enter the *keddah* or
stockade to calm the
captured wild elephants.
When the required wild
elephants have been
selected they are securely
roped to tame ones (below).
Interested foreigners, in
solar topis, survey the
heaving sea of elephant
backs from ringside seats.

soothing effect upon them. The mahouts cleverly steered their elephants so that individual members were gradually separated from the herd. In each case, a tame elephant moved in close and as it did so, the man behind the mahout slipped to the ground with his rope. Then he hit the wild elephant's hindleg and as it was raised in protest he quickly slipped a noose over it and pulled it tight. The other end of the rope was then pulled by the tame elephant and by degrees the unfortunate prisoner was hauled to a nearby tree where it was firmly secured.

The lengthy operation of tethering all the elephants was usually conducted with great efficiency, for the mahouts were experienced at approaching closely without causing too many upsets. The only really dangerous moments were when females were separated from their calves. On these occasions they ran blindly in search of their offspring, roaring, attacking, and whipping

others around them into a similar frenzy of nervous exhaustion. At such times the mahouts backed off until mother and offspring were re-united and the calm they required to carry out their work had again returned to the stockade.

When the job was done the elephants were left in peace to settle down. They were, of course, by then furious at being roped to a tree and not a little alarmed by the disruption of their social grouping. At the slightest approach they reared up bellow-

Right: An illustration of 1892 shows a herd of wild elephants trapped as the stockade gate drops, portcullis-like, behind them.

ing with rage and fear, ensuring that their captors remained at a respectable distance. Only when their need for food and water became acute did they show any signs of co-operation. Once replenished, however, the wilder side of their nature appeared once more.

After two or three days, when the elephants had begun to feed more peacefully, it became safer to attempt to move them to their place of training. This was never an easy task, for the wild elephant would have been looking for every opportunity to make its getaway to the safety of the forest. To control it, one or two tame elephants were roped to it and it was marched off in an undignified fashion to an encampment. Once there, it was installed between other tame elephants whose role was to demonstrate the friendliness of the men in charge, and of one man in particular.

Turning to the problems and procedures of elephant training today, one again finds time-honored methods in use. Probably the most important aspect of elephant training was, and still is, that of giving the responsibility of an individual elephant to one man. The elephant will readily respond to a single mahout, with whom lies the responsibility for building up a solid working relationship based on mutual trust.

Those animals approaching their twentieth year are the most economical to train because they are within only a few years of peak fitness and can be set to work on strenuous tasks within a relatively short time of their capture. On the other hand, these individuals have also attained their independence by the time they are rounded up and are approaching their sexual prime. They do not take lightly to being denied the freedom of the forests. The mahout works with careful understanding, exploiting the natural instinct of his elephant to form a relationship of trust.

There are many instances of mahouts who have opted to beat their captives into submission, cruelly punishing them for their mistakes and inability to respond quickly and efficiently to the first harsh orders. Such animals will work, but their days toil is generally marred by their resentment of their handling and they often become bad tempered and dangerous.

The most obvious ploy, and the one usually adopted, is to mitigate with kindness and sympathy the traumatic change in living conditions so suddenly imposed upon the giant creatures. However the mahout must still gain the upper hand in the battle between brain and brawn. He confronts his elephant as early as he can, talking to it in a soothing way, though also using a sharply pointed stick (called a *hawkus*) to punish the trunk. It soon learns that such unruly behavior results in a sharp prick of pain and before long the vulnerable trunk is held obediently in place. But if fear is used initially to suppress the

Above: An elephant scissors two logs between tusks and trunk, with impressive balance.

Above: A young elephant lowers its head to gain better purchase on a log.

elephant's untamed spirit, it is not long before it is rewarded for its submission. Food is plentiful and each day it will be taken to bathe. Although the tame elephants remain in close attendance and the mahout still threatens to use his sharp, metal point the trainee soon learns to take the easy way, to eat its fill and indulge gratefully in one of its most favored pastimes, bathing.

After several weeks of discipline the tame elephants are no longer required and the lightly-hobbled apprentice is controlled by the single mahout who needs to do little more than offer the point of his weapon should the elephant show persistent signs of breaking its routines.

It is the special privilege of the mahout to name his elephant. The animal will not be expected to respond to this identification but names are given so that the men can talk about their elephants among themselves. Thus, the names have more human value than anything else, becoming descriptive of the qualities of the elephant – perhaps its emotional or physical attributes, or even telling of some special association or of an act of courage. Thus, Ma Shwe's daughter of the raging river was known as Miss Laughing Water and in the same book, *Elephant Bill*, we find Kya M'Nine (The tiger could not overthrow him), Ma Pin Wa (Miss Fat Bottom), Ma Hla (Miss Pretty), Maung Kyaw Dan (Mr Straight-back) and, rare compliment indeed, Bandoola who was named after a famous general who served in the First Burmese War against the British in the 1820s.

Once the young elephant has been brought under control and is considered sufficiently safe and trustworthy, the mahout introduces it to the idea of being ridden. This is not an easy task for much of the earlier treatment will have relied upon using and adapting the natural attributes of the elephant to best advantage, particularly its ability to form strong relationships. Now the animal is introduced to procedures which are more alien to it.

The best time to accustom the elephant to bearing a human on its neck, immediately behind its great ears, is often considerable when it is on the point of cutting its ties with its mother. The adult, her role nearly over, will not be too resentful and the calf, at around five years of age, will still be young and playful enough to accept more lightly the burden of its load. Of course, it is not always possible for it to happen this way for many of the elephants required for work will have been captured when they are fully independent. But the principle remains the same, albeit a more tricky process in the older elephants.

The mahout (or *oozie* as he is referred to in Burma) leads his trainee to a special enclosure, enticing it to enter with offerings of fruit and words of reassurance. Once safely installed in its pen, like a bull before its release into the open ring, the elephant often becomes suspicious and attempts to break out. Its nerves are calmed by more fruit and the presence of other, older tame elephants. While the newcomer is settling down, the mahout is hauled on a pulley way up over its head. He is slowly lowered on to the back of its neck. The elephant often reacts violently and throws the mahout off. This procedure is repeated many times. Each time the elephant is rewarded with a banana. The routine continues until the

The lives of working elephants are similar throughout the countries of Asia. In Sri Lanka (opposite) a bath and scrub marks the welcome end of the day's work. At Munnar in south India (left) an elephant sets off to work on a tea estate, carrying foliage to consume later. In Thailand (below) an elephant struggles to grip the dry earth with its feet as it pulls huge logs of wood.

elephant grows used to the presence of a load upon its head.

Meanwhile, a heavy block of padded wood, heavier than the elephant can support, is suspended above the middle of the elephant's back and is eventually lowered gently into place. The elephant generally struggles all the more and the block is lifted away but descends again a few minutes later. Finally, in desperation, the elephant collapses to the ground, its front legs stretched out in the limited space ahead of its weary body.

In *Elephant Bill*, Williams describes the training process: 'A cheer goes up from the Burmans: a cheer which soon becomes a chant of "Tah!" (Get up) "Hmit!" (Sit down). As the weight is lifted, the calf gets up, and all the Burmans chant, "Tah!" As the weight comes down, and the calf sits, all of them chant. "Hmit!" in chorus.

After a time the rider, still attached to the pulley, remains comfortably seated on its head. By evening, unless the calf is a really obstinate young devil, the rider can turn and, putting his hand on its back instead of the log of wood, order the calf to sit down by pressure and by saying, "Hmit!"

Once that is possible, the calf is considered broken. Often it takes less than twelve hours, with no cruelty whatsoever. Sometimes, however, when dealing with obstinate and truculent young tuskers, the game has to be kept up, by the light of bamboo torches, far into the night.'

Even when officially 'broken,' the elephant is still many long years away from the great forests

Above: A mahout props up his *ankus* or *hawkus* – the hooked metal rod used to give commands to his elephant – during a heavy job.

Above: Two young friends drink on a hot afternoon beside the tumbling river.

Above: A co-ordinated joint effort is needed as two elephants make a pile of logs.

Above: Wooden bells round the necks of these Thai elephants clink as they bathe.

Leaping and jumping elephants in this old print of a steeplechase in Rangoon c1858, betray artistic license — for elephants cannot spring.

where it will spend 30 or more years hauling logs. It goes immediately to a special nursery where its treatment is relatively gentle, its relationship with the mahout or oozie develops, and the elephant is taught to respond to more everyday commands and to accustom itself more fully to the presence of a rider behind its head.

By moving his body to the right or left or by applying pressure with his feet to the sensitive areas behind the elephant's ears, the mahout can induce steering responses, and within a short time the elephant will turn, or kneel down in response to the mahout's pressure pushing down the back of its head. By exerting pressure with the foot to the side of the elephant's neck it may be taught to raise the appropriate leg. Some three years later, the strengthening elephant will be given its first light loads to carry. These will never be much, for elephants are not good at actually carrying weights of more than a few hundred pounds. Their main strength lies in pulling dead weights that a dozen men or more could never move.

Perhaps 10 years elapse, the elephant learning all the time and growing toward the day when, devoted to its master and responding well to every touch and word of command, it is ready to join a work-force in the huge forests of Southeast Asia where the ever-increasing rate of tree-felling will keep it busy for the rest of its healthy life.

In *Elephant Bill* Williams gives a detailed resumé of the economics and logistics of elephant training in Burma between the two world wars:

'During the early years the elephant never really earns its keep or does enough to pay the wages of its oozie, but is learning all the time. By the time it is nineteen its temperament is fully known, and it has developed physically sufficiently for its future values as a working animal to be gauged.

Up to the age of nineteen or twenty it will have cost about one thousand pounds, when the wages of the oozie, training costs and maintenance are added up. Any earning capacity it might have had during those years would be small, even if used for rice transport. Moreover, any attempt to increase its earnings during the early years is very bad policy, and likely to involve its being overloaded and its whole future usefulness put in jeopardy. We may assume that the elephant has on the average a working life from its twentieth to its fifty-fifth year. In this period it may cost another one thousand five hundred pounds in the wages of its oozie and in maintenance.

Each working year consists of nine months' work and three months' rest, necessary both to keep it in condition, and on account of the seasonal changes. From June to the end of February are the working months; whilst during the hot weather season from March to May, animals

Right: Times change and although their elephants were not trained for work like this, local mahouts are glad of the money that tourists will pay to have their picture taken on an elephant's back.

Above: Nearly missed the bus! A latecomer scrambles on board as the local transport gets under way.

should not work, there being insufficient fodder and water for them in the teak-bearing and deciduous forest areas.

Each month consists of only eighteen working days and twelve rest days, animals working three days in succession and then resting two. Thus, during the nine months of the working year there are only 162 working days. Each day averages about eight hours. Thus an elephant works 1,300 a year. During this time an average animal delivers 100 tons of timber from stump to a floating-point in a creek. This is only one of the steps in the transport of the teak to the mill.'

A small calculation shows that an elephant working for 30 years will not only complete in the region of 20,000 hours of labor (a man working seven hours a day for 40 years will complete from 50,000 to 60,000 hours in his life) but will also be party to the removal of about 3000 tons of wood from the forests. Obviously, such a removal cannot be tolerated for long but it is a tragic irony that when the forests have gone, and the wild elephants with them, they will, in fact, have expended this use for working elephants.

At some stage in the capturing of wild elephants it evidently occurred to the captors that their best policy, based on the herding tendency of their quarry, would be to round up hundreds of elephants at a time. They could then select, unharmed, all those of use and even afford themselves the luxury of setting free those of no use to them. It was a successful ploy that was to lead not only to massive numbers of elephants working in the forests but also to the wholesale use of elephants as formidable vehicles of war. Indeed, the latter reason was quite likely the first one that led to the formation of plans for capture on such a massive scale. To amass an army of elephants obviously demanded a great deal of

Above: Elephants and men alike must stop for rest and refreshment as the midday heat hazes the air.

Above: Painted, draped, and accompanied by a local musician, an elephant carries travellers to Amber Fort near Jaipur in India.

Right: The war elephant portrayed in this medieval manuscript painting is carrying an impossibly large fortress full of quarrelsome knights, armed with all manner of weapons. The drawing of the animal is remarkably accurate, however, indicating that the artist had actually seen this rare creature, or had had information from a trader travelling in the East or a soldier from a Crusade.

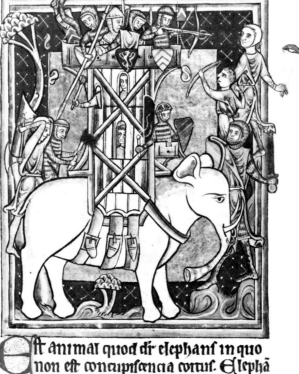

capturing and training, or at least many years of breeding the right animals in captivity. It was not surprising, therefore, that a large number of domestic elephants was something of a rarity and that the strength of a particular army was often assessed in terms of its elephant force alone. At exactly what period in history the use of war elephants arose is not certain but it seems that it may have begun in Asia. By 500 BC, the use of war elephants was widespread in the Middle East. The Assyrian Queen Semiramis is said to have used dummies of elephants mounted on camels when she moved eastward to attack India in the ninth century BC. She must have realized the psychological effect of advancing elephants.

A typical war elephant would be furnished with five plates of iron joined together by rings and fastened around the elephant's ears and head by a complex of chains. As if this was not enough weight for an animal renowned for its inability to carry great burdens (despite a known strength capable of pushing and pulling weights, the elephant has very weak shoulders), there would be a wooden castle (equivalent to a howdah) on its back. It housed a number of archers and spearmen. In the first book of Maccabees, in the Apocrypha, the use of war elephants in the second century BC is well described (though the quoted number of 32 soldiers riding on each animal, in addition to the Indian mahout, sounds like an exaggeration. It would hardly be possible for an elephant to stand up under such a load, let alone march into battle with an exuberance calculated to put the enemy to flight.)

In his account about his famous journey to the East, Marco Polo (the thirteenth-century Venetian explorer) tells of Kublai Khan riding into battle in a large wooden castle built across the backs of four elephants standing side by side. Their flanks were protected by thick leather skirts decorated in bright colors. Their heads were encased with armor from which loomed the pearl-white splendor of magnificent tusks. An armed soldier – in control of the fearsome beasts – sat on each of their necks immediately in front of the castle which was itself a formidable piece of military equipment. The upper compartment, flying the imperial standard, contained not only the great man himself, the Mongul emperor, but also a score of archers who could send showers of arrows down on the enemy.

Perhaps the most famous account of the use of elephants in war concerns Hannibal, the Carthaginian general (this will be discussed in Chapter 5), but, possibly the best documented example of the military deployment of elephants relates to Alexander the Great as told by the Greek historian, Arrian. It is famous because it concerns the defeat of an army dependent upon elephants as its major force.

In 326 BC Alexander fought Porus, King of the Punjab of India, at the Battle of the Jhelum River. Alexander had already encountered the use of elephants by the enemy, particularly when fighting Darius, the Persian king who had managed to build up a small reserve from his own military excursions further east. Alexander even had a few elephants with him then, made up of a handful of stragglers from the Indian army and some 25 presented to him by the Rajah of Taxila in return for military aid.

Here Alexander and his war-weary Macedonian troops faced the intimidating spectacle of a line of more than 200 elephants positioned in front of a massive infantry, flanked on either side by chariots and cavalry. The advantage lay heavily with Porus for not only had he shaken the morale of the Macedonians but the latter also had to cross the swollen River Jhelum. In anticipation of his enemy's next move, Porus dispatched a force of elephants and soldiers to guard the nearest bridge at Haranpur and it seemed that Alexander was trapped. When news filtered through that the Rajah of Kashmir was on his way to help Porus, Alexander resorted to a brilliant tactic. He rushed his army upstream to a distant bridge at Jalalpur and crossed the swollen river at night. Without resting his men and under the discomfort and yet cover of a downpour of rain, he advanced on Porus' unsuspecting army.

With the odds against him reduced considerably, Alexander was now able to apply his considerable skills against the main force of elephants ahead of him. He would not be drawn into them easily, for he knew that his horses and men, tired and rainsodden, would panic in the face of such a formidable opposition and the day would be lost.

Instead, he formed a large circle around the elephants and ordered his archers to pick off the mahouts and the soldiers riding on their backs. Then, to drive the elephants out of control, his men hit them with spears and arrows so that they broke rank and charged wildly. The Macedonians found themselves too close to escape the fury they had provoked and many of them were crushed underfoot. However Porus' men also suffered the same fate and before they could restore any order

Left: An engraving of 1785 shows an elephant whose odd eyes, trunk tips and feet indicate that the artist's references were inadequate. To add to the slightly fantastic impression, a very graceful mahout seems to be gently scratching his elephant's head with his *ankus* (training rod).

Above: In the past, elephant fighting was a popular sport. This historic painting shows two elephants in violent combat, goaded by their mahouts and further provoked by spectators waving rods with exploding fireworks at their ends.

Alexander's infantry came in from all directions and hacked away at the elephants with spears, knives, and curved scythes. Tails, tendons, and trunks lay scattered on a battlefield discolored by the copious blood of trampled victims. The more that Porus' men were driven back, the greater their number destroyed by their own elephants. It was a magnificent victory for Alexander, but it was also one that took its toll of lives.

Yet, the victorious Macedonian troops suffered greatly themselves. They had challenged and defeated the might of an elephant army from the East, but their nerves had broken under the strain. They vowed that not even under the command of their greatest leader would they ever face an elephant army again.

King Porus was taken prisoner suffering from nine wounds received during the rout of his defenses. Although his victory was a bloody one, Alexander was in many ways a compassionate man. He had been greatly impressed by the might and splendor of the opposition against him and now he set Porus free, allowing him to retain his kingdom and even adding more land to it. It is said that a medal bearing Alexander's elephant-skin clad head was specially made in memory of this spectacular victory.

Alexander was to die some three years after this war. His empire was divided and soon a long war between Asia and Egypt was underway. Both sides used elephants to some effect but because they were far removed from breeding stocks in the East, and as Alexander had demonstrated the vulnerability of the elephant in battle, they were gradually used less and less. Attempts were made to import and train African elephants for warfare but these enjoyed only a small amount of the success of their eastern relatives.

The final demise of the Asian elephant as a creature of war in the West (they were used in the siege of Colombo, in the East, in 1588) did not actually come about for over a thousand years. W Boyd Dawkins and H W Oakley, writing in Cassell's nineteenth-century *Natural History* in-

clude the following passage which details a late example of war elephants in action:

'When Timour, or Tamerlane, attacked the dominions of the Sultan Mahmoud (AD 1399), the Elephants, of which the latter had a considerable number, caused great terror and alarm and that the preparations made by Timour to overcome the Elephants were of the most extraordinary nature, for not only did he surround his camp with a deep ditch and bucklers, but also had Buffaloes tied together round the ramparts, with huge brambles on their heads, which were to be set on fire at the approach of the Elephants. The forces of the Sultan, besides the Elephants, consisted of a large number of horse and foot soldiers armed with swords and poisoned daggers. Atten-

Above: With the snowclad peaks of the Himalayas in the distance, an elephant carries an umbrella-shaded couple across the Rapti River at Chitwan in Nepal.

Above: Marco Polo, the Venetian explorer, c 1254–1323, was among the first to bring to Europe tales of fabulous elephants, especially those he saw at the court of the Mongol emperor, Kublai Khan.

dant upon the Elephants were men armed with fire, melted pitch and other horrid missiles, to be hurled at the invaders. The Elephants also, besides being armed were decorated with all sorts of articles, such as cymbals and bells, and other objects likely to create a noise and confusion. Notwithstanding all this terrific display, Timour's forces fought with great courage, actually defeating the Sultan's forces and putting the Elephants to flight, the unfortunate creatures undergoing severe usage to their trunks by the swordsmen, who appeared soon to find out the more vulnerable parts. It is said that the trunks of many of the Elephants were left scattered on the battle-field having been severed by the sword. The belief in the invincibility of the Elephants was then for ever gone; and it is even said of Timour's grandson, then quite a boy, that he himself wounded an Elephant, and drove it in as a captive to his grandfather's camp.'

The deciding factor in the decline of elephants as war machines was the invention of firearms. Elephants are generally startled by the report of a gun and tend to panic under such pressure. It would have been a relatively simple matter to dispatch a handful of men to fire into the midst of a herd of elephants and cause them to panic and

Above: Kublai Khan riding to war in his elephant car – a contemporary artist's impression, based on the writings of Marco Polo.

unleash the fury intended for the enemy upon their own ranks. A strategic counterpart of the elephant later emerged – the tank, which performed a role comparable to that played by the elephant, running ahead of the main body of men, destroying everything in its path, and undermining the morale of the enemy.

However if the elephant was made redundant as a machine of war, its image lived on in the minds of the humans of Southeast Asia. It was several thousand years ago that its great strength and placid nature were first harnessed by man. Out of this relationship grew a reverence, and a respect which assured great prestige for the owners of elephants – especially white elephants. The beasts were decorated and paraded for all to see and admire. The graceful sweeps of the solid body lent themselves to artists who carved them out of wood and stone, and by degrees they were incorporated into religious beliefs and ceremonies. The elephant as an art form or as a symbol of religion is as

Below: A war elephant dashes a writhing warrior to pieces against the ground. This statue is in the compound of the temple of the sun god at Konarak in the State of Orissa, India.

Below: From a shrine of wood carved in relief and decoratively painted, the god Ganesha surveys the world with pot-bellied wisdom and a merry wit.

Right: A worshipper prays to a gilded Ganesha, asking the god to remove obstacles to his chosen path in life.

The elephant–headed god

Ganesh or Ganesha is one of the best-known of the Hindu gods, and his elephant-headed effigy is usually found guarding the door of shrines sacred to Shiva. This alludes to his power to remove obstacles to one's true purpose; on temples and shrines he represents the removal of any hindrance to true worship and spiritual enlightenment. Ganesh is the god of intelligence, and hence the patron of students and teachers.

In Hindu mythology, Ganesh was the son of the goddess Parvati. He would stand at her door to protect her privacy while she was at her toilet. One day the god Shiva tried to enter; when he was repelled by Ganesh he called on Vishnu, who sent a comely young female spirit to distract Ganesh. One of Shiva's demons cut off Ganesh's head and Shiva entered. Parvati was so furious, however, that Shiva placated her by promising to restore life to her son. He sent his guards to bring back the first head they could find, which was that of an elephant.

Ganesh is usually shown in a pot-bellied, merry attitude; folk stories show that he has a zest for good living, and a cunning wit.

strong in the East today as it ever was. It stands proudly on many a temple, gateway or non-religious building and decorates countless tiled floors, walls, and ceilings.

The great Hindu god of wisdom and good fortune, Ganesha, probably embodies the mind and soul of the elephant today in the East more than anything else. Ganesha, which has the body of a man supporting the head of an elephant, is the product of a fascinating piece of history.

Ganesha, the son of the goddess Parvati, prevented Shiva, the Prince of Demons, from entering his mother's house. In his thwarted fury, Shiva struck Ganesha's head to the ground with the ominous oath that it should be restored in the shape of the head of the first nonhuman animal to appear. This, of course, was an elephant. So Ganesha went his way, riding on a rat and begging for his food. He acquired a reputation for his human intelligence and his elephant wisdom.

One night, so the story goes, he indulged in too much rice and his belly swelled enormously. When confronted with a dangerous snake which loomed out of the light of the moon, the rat bolted for safety and threw Ganesha to the ground with such force that his distended belly burst. The snake, by now Ganesha's prisoner, was required to make good the damage it had caused. When this was done the night sky blackened and was filled with the echoings of the moon that was said to have rocked with laughter at the scene below. So great was Ganesha's fury, so hurt was his pride, that he tore out one of his tusks and hurled it at the moon. It is because of this act, they still say, that the moon regularly has a portion missing from its side.

The elephant is deeply rooted in the traditions of Eastern life and nowhere more deeply than in the lives of royalty. The preparation of the royal elephants for stately occasions was a lavish affair. They would be bathed in pure water and then liberally doused with eastern perfumes. Once their hides were dry and smelling sweet, artists would set to work, carefully painting their heads and ears with brilliant colors in shapes following the solid contours of their bones beneath. The tusks were scrubbed clean and adorned with gold. When the paint was dry, a splendid cloak of royal scarlet, gold, purple, and yellow was spread across the back. When the final trimmings of necklaces and pendants were all in place, the full splendor of the animal and its proud mahout were paraded in public for the gathered throngs.

Today it is a sad reflection that such pageantry is becoming a thing of the past. The elephant is now used less than ever in matters of state. However, one may suppose that the cult of the elephant will never die, and in one way they are still very much a part of the present – as work animals.

Tiger!

The sport of tiger hunting was the delight of Indian princes and maharajahs for centuries, and later became one of the grand events in the gilded era of the British Raj. The elephant was the ideal mount for tiger-hunting parties. In a comfortable howdah strapped to the elephant's back, the hunter had excellent mobility through tangled jungle or tall grass and bamboo thickets; he also had a perfect viewpoint from which to sight and aim at his quarry. The size of the elephants gave the hunter the illusion, at least, of safety from the savage tiger, although incidents such as the one portrayed (right) cannot have been uncommon. The elephants were trained for particular obedience and steadfastness in the face of danger, although in a large hunting party the sheer number of elephants, pitted against one or two tigers, made the combat pitifully unequal.

With the coming of more sophisticated and accurate firearms in the last century, Indian tigers were killed in stupendous numbers: just one maharajah killed well over a thousand tigers during his life. (Numbers of elephants killed in such hunts were not considered important enough to be recorded.) The Victorian empire-builders enthusiastically joined in this exotic native sport, and elephant-mounted tiger hunts were one of the lavish entertainments offered to visiting royalty such as the Prince of Wales. More recently, rugged overland vehicles, with spotlights for night hunting, replaced elephants in the tiger hunt, but only the most rapid and effective conservation methods can now save the tiger.

Right: The Duc d'Orleans displays truly aristocratic sang-froid during a hair-raising incident while tiger hunting in Nepal. A wounded and enraged tiger makes a leap on to the elephant's back, apparently breaking the duke's gun with one strike of its huge paw.

Below left: The then Prince of Wales (left) who would have been crowned Edward VIII but for his abdication, was one of the royal visitors to India who participated in a tiger hunt on elephants.

Left: Another Prince of Wales, another tiger hunt: this one, the son of Queen Victoria and later to be Edward VII, was on a state visit to India in 1875–76.

Left: A caparisoned elephant bears the god Rama and his half-brother Lakshman in procession through Old Delhi. This annual festival of Ramlila commemorates the slaying of the demon king of Lanka (now Sri Lanka). The Hindu religious epic is acted out in a series of plays in the ancient sacred cities of India.

Left: Sparkling in the night, ceremonial elephants carry a relic of Buddha through the town of Kelaniya, near Colombo, Sri Lanka. The electric lights adorning the elephants and the reliquary shrine are powered by a small generator being towed behind the elephants.

Opposite: Elephants seem to show little resentment at being painted and decorated, perhaps even enjoying the fuss and excitement. This one, masked in fluttering white cotton, waits with his mahout (also in best dress) for the beginning of a procession in Kandy, Sri Lanka.

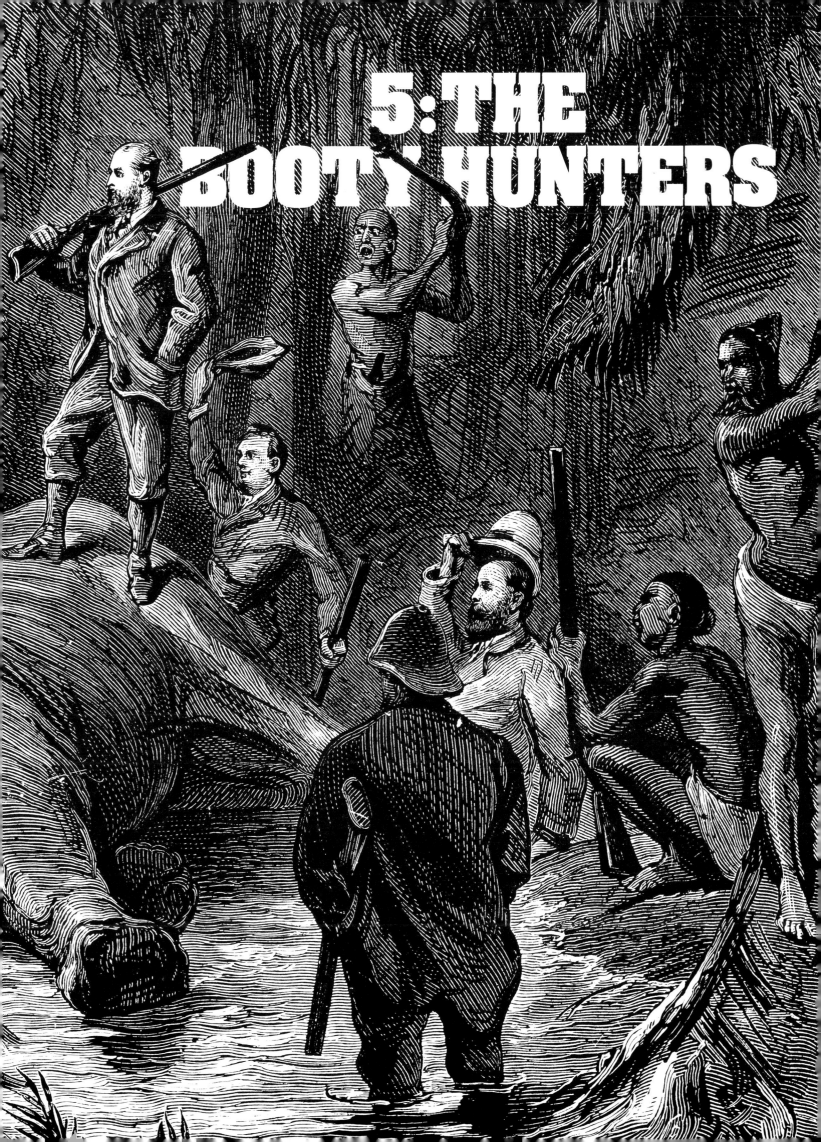

5: THE BOOTY HUNTERS

Previous page: The Prince of Wales, on his State Visit to India in 1875–76, poses for an admiring audience on top of an elephant he has just bagged – no doubt with a little help from his friends.

Below: Even before the coming of the white man, ivory was used by African tribesmen, such as this old man in Togo blowing a horn made from an elephant tusk.

It now seems almost certain that man evolved in Africa. Should this be proven, then also it will be shown beyond any doubt – despite the cult of the elephant in the East – that it was on that continent that man's first encounters with elephant-like animals took place. Even now, the evidence suggests that African elephants were being captured and trained long before those from the East. Exploitation of the African elephant has never really ceased, and this century has seen an intensification of the traffic in a way unknown to the ancient world. For the African elephant has been hunted remorselessly for its ivory, bringing the species to the verge of extinction. Looking first into the remote past raises a problem. In past centuries African elephants were used domestically and in war. Yet today it is accepted that African elephants cannot be trained, that their natures are such that they are unmanageable in captivity. Witness the abundance of Asian ele-

phants in zoos and circuses the world over and their commercial exploitation in the Far East. So what was it that made the African elephant manageable two or three thousand years ago but not today?

The answer lies almost certainly with the kind of elephant used. When we think of the African elephant today it is the large bush elephant which figures in our minds, the master of the savannahs with its huge ears, gleaming tusks, and a willingness – albeit a mistaken impression – to charge at anything on sight. There is, of course, an element of truth in this. Out on the plains the pressures from predators is intense and all animals have developed acute senses to warn them of potential danger. They feed primed and ready to make a fleet-footed escape, to merge with their surroundings or even to stand and fight. It is not surprising that the bush elephant has earned itself a reputation for a certain ugliness of character.

Left: Delicately carved combs and rings, thousands of years old, bear witness to the availability and use of ivory in predynastic Egypt.

But consider the elephant – of a different subspecies as we have already seen in the first chapters – which lives not in the open savannahs but in forests on the western side of the continent. There, under cover of dense vegetation, it lives in small social groups without fear of its vulnerably sized calves being spotted by a lionness or a pack of hyenas some hundreds of yards away. At the slightest provocation it can move silently to a safe place only a handful of paces from where it was first disturbed. No need to turn and charge.

The significance of this could be that the smaller elephant of the forests has evolved a less temperamental nature than its open-country counterpart and that this factor alone predisposed it to being more amenable to the captive company of human beings.

The Asian elephant is essentially an animal of forests as well and it falls into the same category. Thus, it seems that some 3000 years ago, elephants in Africa, particularly the forest elephants, were far more widespread than they are today. They ranged along the northern shores, in present day Morocco and Tunisia, where they inhabited forested and mountainous regions. It was probably these forest elephants of Africa that were first captured by man. As a result, they have become quite rare.

The evidence to support this suggestion is quite good. The elephants which occupied the northwestern coast of Africa, along the Atlantic Ocean, the northern forests, and even the Nile Valley in the east formed an (almost) continuous population of which the remnants are today found in West Africa alone. They were small animals by contemporary elephant proportions, a fact deduced from the relative size of the elephants and their riders as depicted on formal seals of office. Of course, it would have been possible for the scale to have been unrepresentative of reality, but there is a persuasive consistency about these illustrations. It is therefore reasonable to assume that the earliest references to the relationship between man and the African elephant concern the forest elephant alone.

The very first records, dating back some 6000 years, are of ivory which was collected from the northern shores of Africa and used principally by the Egyptians for carvings. (This was probably a much older tradition, indeed there is even a record of a small group of figures carved out of mammoth ivory in Europe some 20,000 years ago.) Later records show that elephant hunting – as opposed to elephant capturing – was common along the lush banks of the Nile as early as 1500 BC, although there are various indications that they were actually caught for private collections as much as 3000 years ago. Aristotle, from his own dissections, made detailed anatomical observations on elephants during the fourth century BC and he even published in his *Historia Animalium* recognized techniques for elephant hunting and capturing by a primitive method of rounding-up the animals.

But such records as these are far from hard proof that the African elephant was domesticated and used by man on a serious scale. The first real evidence for this arises in the story of Alexander the Great mentioned in the previous chapter. After Alexander's death in 323 BC the Asian war elephants declined in number and attentions were turned toward their African counterparts.

Ptolemy Philadelphus – the second of the Ptolemaic rulers who vied for the remnants of Alexander's empire – sent various expeditions to the riverine areas of North Africa, to such regions

Training the forest elephant

Below: Orderly and submissive, a group of trained forest elephants take the parade at the training station of Gangala-na-Bodio in the former Belgian Congo, in 1948. Their small size, slender heads, and long, slim tusks distinguish them from bush elephants.

It is a common error to assume that African elephants cannot be domesticated. In fact the African forest elephant, unlike its better-known and larger cousin the African bush elephant, can be tamed and trained as easily as the Asian elephant. There may be several reasons why forest elephants have not been more widely domesticated: perhaps their relatively low numbers, the difficulty of capturing them in the jungle, or simply that the native human populations of the region have no urgent necessity for trained elephants.

However, as these pictures, taken in 1948 demonstrate, forest elephants have been successfully trained in the Belgian Congo. The first elephant training station was started at Kiravunga in the Uele region in 1899 by the Belgian Commandant Laplume, on the orders of King Leopold of Belgium. In 1930 the main training station was opened at Gangala-na-Bodio. These pictures show the capture, training and use of elephants from this base.

Wild elephants were captured with rope lassoes and subdued with the help of specially trained domesticated elephants. Training methods were similar to those practiced for centuries in Asia. Once trained, the elephants were hired out for ground clearance, haulage and tree-felling, being allowed the freedom of the local forest when not working. Despite the success of this station (largely due to the dedication of the Belgian Commandant) none other like it was ever opened in forest elephant territory in Africa.

Above: At the end of his tether — a wild forest elephant struggles against the ropes that restrain him.

Above: Chained and frightened, a forest elephant wheels to trumpet his defiance at his Congolese captors.

African forest elephants (fully grown but still small by elephant standards) are boarded, with some difficulty, on to a steamer for transport to a training station. These fascinating pictures, taken several decades ago, remain a tantalizing glimpse of colonial Africa, and a record of an experiment in training elephants that, despite its success, has not been widely repeated.

Right: The Greek philosopher Aristotle dissected and described elephants in the fourth century BC.

Right: A cameo of sardonyx portrays Ptolemy II with his wife. He organized the capture and use of elephants in North Africa.

that we know today as Eritrea, Sudan, and Ethiopia. Here elephants were found in great numbers and in 280 BC a port for their shipment abroad was established. It was called Ptolemais Theron, meaning 'Ptolemais of the Hunts.' The elephants were driven to the coast and loaded, with some difficulty, on to ships. On these they sailed up the Red Sea to the port of Berenice from where they marched across the scorching desert to their new home in the Nile Valley. There is no evidence to suggest how these elephants were captured or even trained but there were mahouts available who had dealt with the Asian elephants and it is likely that they simply switched their attentions to the new animals when they arrived. Ptolemy used his new weapon effectively and was able to secure a number of important victories.

However, the real test of the African elephant in war was still to come. In 217 BC Ptolemy IV, with his elephants from Africa, engaged the Asian elephants of Antiochus the Great of Syria. Ptolemy may have won the day with a superior show of overall strength but his elephants were put to military shame by the superiority of the Asian animals. It has been written that the smaller African elephant – another clue to its forest identity – was of a more nervous disposition than its adversary and was not so strong. Although potentially of the same temperament as the Asian elephant, the African elephants may have suffered stress at their capture, transportation, and subsequent training for battle, and these may have been important factors contributing to their failure to live up to expectations in the height of battle. (It is well known in the East that to train an elephant to co-operate fully it has to be caught at the right time and treated very carefully long before it is ready to work at maximum efficiency.)

The Carthaginians of North Africa had an association with African elephants stretching back for centuries and they were able to employ the animals against the occupying Romans, especially in the Punic wars, with notable success. The Romans had had no experience with the beasts. In 255 BC Regulus marched a close-packed contingent of soldiers to fight against the Carthaginian general Xantippus only to find his troops annihilated by the steam-roller impact of an advancing band of elephants. Hannibal, the most famous Carthaginian, was able to embark upon one of the best-known – and one of the most successful – of all war programs involving elephants.

Hannibal grew up with the knowledge that elephants could be used in war and he would have had plenty of time to understand their ways in captivity. When he witnessed the inability of the Romans to deal with them he formulated a plan that was as ambitious as it was bold. He decided to march both elephants and soldiers on Rome, to

Above: Defying rugged terrain and hostile weather, Hannibal took elephants over the Alps in a daring and successful bid against Roman power.

Above: Hannibal's elephants bear down on the Roman troops of Scipio Africanus at the Battle of Zama, fought 85 miles from Carthage in 202 BC.

Above: Captive elephants, set against Jewish prisoners in the Roman theater at Alexandria, cause more damage among the spectators.

capture the city and free his people of the Roman yoke.

During the Second Punic War (c 219–202 BC), Hannibal set off through Spain with 15,000 foot soldiers and a rather small contingent of 37 elephants. He crossed the Pyrenees and then trekked northeastward through France, crossing the Rhône without losing a single animal. Exactly how he accomplished the feat is not precisely clear and various accounts exist. One narrative states, that the fiercest elephant was provoked by its keeper to such an extent that, when the intrepid man dived into the water, his elephant dived in after him and was immediately followed by the rest of the herd, which swam the width of the Rhône in safety.

Another more credible account appears in Cassell's *Natural History*, an adaptation of Polybius:

'It is said that one raft two hundred feet long and fifty broad was extended from the bank to the river, and was then secured higher up by several strong cables to the bank, that it might not be carried down by the stream. The soldiers then covered it over with earth, so that the animals might tread upon it without fear, as on solid ground. Another raft – one hundred feet long, and of the same breadth as the other, was joined to this first. The elephants were driven along the stationary raft as along a road, and then, the females leading the way, passed on to the other raft, which was fastened to it by lashings. This, on being cut, was drawn by boats to the opposite shore. The elephants gave no signs whatever of alarm, while they were driven along as it were on a continuous bridge; but a few became infuriated when the raft was let loose, and fell into the river, finding their way, however, safely to the shore.'

At this stage it was remarkable enough that Hannibal had managed to keep his numbers virtually intact, but now the daunting prospect of crossing the Alps loomed ahead. Unperturbed, he drove man and beast into the rugged terrain with its glaciers, precipices, and constant threats of avalanches. They were subjected to bitterly cold temperatures by night and their vision was obscured by low clouds by day. They could take only the easiest contours, hoping to find a pass. But somehow the barrier was crossed and as the foothills of northern Italy came into view, Hannibal had time to assess the consequences of the exploit. No figures are given but many of his men and elephants had succumbed to the rigors of the journey. Although those that remained alive were in desperate need of rest, Hannibal marched them on with confidence. When the Romans were finally confronted with an elephant army at Trebia the battle was won decisively by the Carthaginian whose tactics were too much for an opposition still unable to cope with the legendary

'living tank.' Their horses panicked at the sight and smell of the elephants and their soldiers were too closely grouped to avoid the onslaught. The Roman ranks broke in chaos and Hannibal's men moved in to win the day.

Unfortunately for Hannibal, though, the combination of the journey and the battle was beginning to take serious effect. His men were depleted in both numbers and morale and his brave elephants, exhausted and suffering from the climatic changes involved in travelling from Africa to Europe, were now dying all around him. By the time he reached the Arno River to the south, only one elephant – the one on which he rode himself – remained alive. It was at this stage that Hannibal abandoned his plans to capture Rome.

In a sense it was Hannibal's use of the elephant to confront the Romans that was his people's undoing. By 202 BC the great war leader was back in Carthage and once again using elephants to stem the flow of enemy soldiers into his land. But the Romans had seen enough of such tactics and their general, Scipio Africanus, came armed with the knowledge that his defeated predecessors had lacked. When he met Hannibal in battle he deployed his troops in a way reminiscent of Alexander the Great. He spaced out his ranks and ordered them to aim at the elephants and their riders. The elephants panicked and turned on their own lines of men. As the Roman soldiers moved in they hacked at trunks and bowels, while armored horses and chariots ran between them inflicting more wounds at close quarters. Hannibal fled and the victorious Romans forced a pledge from the Carthaginians that they would never again capture and train elephants for war.

It also meant that the Romans began to use elephants themselves. But somehow their conservative approach to military matters could not quite accommodate the awe-inspiring flamboyancy of colorful pachyderms trundling into battle. Instead, the African elephant became an object of spectacle and idle pleasure. The barbaric uses that it suffered in front of bloodthirsty crowds – who could themselves be appalled by the spectacle laid on for their amusement – was often worse than anything we might imagine today.

'We are told,' reported Cassell's, 'that in ancient times the number of Elephants brought annually from Africa to Rome, to be trained for the cruel and disgusting practice of fighting in the theatre, was very great. It is said of Pompey that, at the dedication of his theatre, no less than five hundred Lions, eighteen Elephants, and a number of armed men, were all at one time in the circus. In the second consulate of Pompey (BC 54) Elephants were opposed, in the circus, to Getulian archers; and, according to Pliny, this exhibition was characterised by some uncommon circumstances.

One of the Elephants, although furious from a wound, is recorded to have seized upon the shields of his adversaries, and to have thrown them in the air with a peculiar movement, doubtless the effect of training, which caused the shields to whirl round before their fall. It is also stated that an Elephant, having been killed by a thrust of a javelin through the eye, the others rushed forward in a general charge to save him, and that on their coming with terrific force against the iron railings, the latter gave way, and several of the spectators were either injured or killed. On another occasion, when some Elephants, with other wild animals, were fighting together in the arena, the spectators so compassionated the unfortunate creatures, who were raising their trunks to heaven and roaring piteously, as if imploring aid of the gods, that they rose from their seats, and, disregarding Pompey's presence, demanded that the Elephants might be spared.'

This extermination of what we can only suppose was the forest elephant in North Africa happened very quickly. In evolutionary terms, of course, it happened almost instantaneously and it ranks today as a perfect example of the careless effect of man upon the world around him.

In the last 200 years or so we have seen the same thing happening to the larger bush elephant further south in Africa. The extermination process is in part due to the pressure of human populations over millennia. But the process has intensified over the last century. European nations invaded Africa to struggle against each other for political and economic supremacy. Arab slavers and ivory traders ravaged the African interior. Later the idea arose that Africa was some sort of a playground where the rich whites could indulge in the mock heroics of the safari.

Many thousands of years ago human beings lived and hunted in Africa but they killed out of necessity. They lived side by side with their prey animals and the one that they prized above all others – for its plentiful meat, skin, teeth, and bones – was the elephant. By the time that Europeans arrived in the continent, the natives were still employing the hunting techniques handed down to them through countless generations. Pitfall traps were among the commonest techniques used and, according to Sir Samuel Baker who travelled in Africa during the nineteenth century, 'the pits are usually about twelve feet long, and three feet broad, by nine deep; these are artfully made, decreasing towards the bottom to the breadth of a foot. The general Elephant route to the drinking-places being blocked up, the animals are diverted by a treacherous path towards the water, the route being intersected by numerous pits, all of which are carefully concealed by sticks and straw, the latter being usually strewn with Elephants' dung, to create a natural effect. Should an Elephant during the night fall through the deceitful surface, his foot becomes jammed in the bottom of the narrow grave, and he labours shoulder-deep, with two feet in the pitfall so fixed that extrication is impossible. Should one animal be thus caught, a sudden panic seizes the rest of the herd, and in their hasty retreat one or more are generally victims to the numerous pits in the vicinity. Once helpless in the pit, they are easily killed with lances.'

Baker also tells of how the elephant hunters, or *aggageers*, of the Hamran tribe (probably of Arab or Nubian origin – they were dark skinned and had long straight hair) used swords for killing their prey. They would set off early in the morning on the tracks of an elephant, 'so as to arrive at their game between the hours of 10 and 12 A.M., at which time it is either asleep or extremely listless, and easy to approach. Should they discover the animal asleep, one of the hunters would creep stealthily towards the head, and with one blow sever the trunk while stretched upon the ground; in which case the Elephant would start upon his feet, while the hunters escaped in the confusion of the moment. The trunk severed would cause a loss of blood sufficient to insure the death of the Elephant within about an hour. On

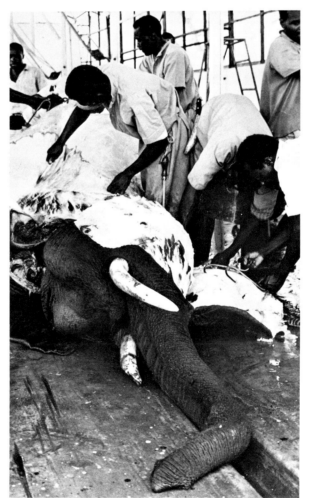

In times past the carcass of an elephant killed in a hunt was divided for food among the hunters, the choice cuts going to the most senior men. After a more recent elephant kill the meat is put into deep-freeze storage for subsequent sale.

Pages from the African diary of a Victorian white hunter: (above) ingenuity comes to the fore as a hunter and his bearer take aim by moonlight, from a raft camouflaged with branches and floated on a lily-decked pool. A wounded elephant (right) causes panic among the natives, who scatter leaving the hunter to kill the enraged animal single-handed.

the other hand, should the animal be awake upon their arrival, it would be impossible to approach the trunk. In such a case, they would creep up from behind, and give a tremendous cut at the back sinew of the hind leg, about a foot above the heel. Such a blow would disable the Elephant at once, and would render comparatively easy a second cut to the remaining leg.'

Such methods as these ensured food for a tribe, but Baker also saw that the sale of the ivory brought in money that enabled hunting techniques to be perfected. More ivory meant more wealth to be used in other ways – for the purchase of food, for instance – and the time was approaching when no more than the tusks of a slaughtered elephant were all of the carcass that was used.

Baker noted that the hunting methods quoted above were for only the poorest hunters and it was not until they had sold their ivory that 'they could purchase Horses for the higher branch of the art. Provided with Horses, the party of hunters could not exceed four. They start before daybreak, and ride slowly throughout the country in search of elephants, generally keeping along the course of a river until they come across the tracks where a herd or a single Elephant, may have drunk during the night. When once upon the track, they follow fast towards the retreating game. The Elephants may be twenty miles distant, but it matters little to the aggageers. At length they discover them, and

the hunt begins. The first step is to single out the bull with the largest tusks; this is the commencement of the fight. After a short hunt, the Elephant turns upon his pursuers, who scatter and fly from his headlong charge until he gives up the pursuit; he at length turns to bay when again pressed by the hunters. It is the duty of one man in particular to ride up close to the head of the Elephant, and thus to absorb its attention upon himself. This insures a desperate charge. The greatest coolness and dexterity are then required by the hunter, who, now the *hunted*, must so adapt the speed of his Horse to the pace of the Elephant, that the enraged beast gains in the race, until it almost reaches the tail of the Horse. In this manner the race continues. In the meantime, two hunters gallop up behind the Elephant, unseen by the animal, whose attention is completely directed to the Horse almost within its grasp. With extreme agility, when close to the heels of the Elephant, one of the hunters, while at full speed, springs to the ground with his drawn sword, as his companion seizes the bridle, and with one dextrous two-handed blow he severs the back sinew. He immediately jumps out of the way, and remounts his Horse; but if the blow is successful, the Elephant is hamstrung, and, as it cannot run rapidly on three legs, is easily killed.'

Once an elephant is dead it is cut up and then the component parts are carefully distributed

Right: Silent and sober, native hunters pose on their victim before cutting up the immense body in a gory ceremony.

Right: In this snapshot for the family album a white hunter records his native trackers dwarfed by the huge tusks of the elephant that they helped him to kill.

among the natives, with priority of choice going to those of seniority in the village and those who have assisted in the hunt, particularly the man who inflicted the first wound.

Gordon Cummings witnessed such a ceremony last century and he has described how the rough outer skin was removed to expose the several layers of rubbery underskin, which was cut off in squares to be made into waterbags. The flesh was then removed in great sheets from the ribs which, when fully exposed, were removed one at a time with hand axes. When each of these colossal pieces of bone had been taken off the carcass, the bowels lay exposed. And it was here that the main interest seemed to focus, for in and around the intestines is a great amount of fat which was highly prized – among some tribes more than in others – for both cooking and eating. To get at it, several men had to enter the open cavity of the elephant's body and work their way round the bowels to the dark interior beyond. It was a messy affair, accompanied by much singing and rejoicing which rose to a fever pitch as the lumps of fat were passed to the outside.

Cummings was awe-struck by the ceremonial activities that took place, noticing in particular that the Bechuana natives' . . . have a horrid practice on these occasions of besmearing their bodies, from the crown of the head to the sole of the foot, with the black and clotted gore; and in this anointing they assist one another, each man taking up the fill of both his hands, and spreading it over the back and shoulders of his friend. Throughout the entire proceeding, an incessant and deafening clamour of many voices and confused sounds is maintained, and violent jostling and wrestling are practised by every man, elbowing the breasts and faces of his fellows, all slippery with gore, as he endeavours to force his way to the flesh through the dense intervening ranks, while the sharp and ready assegai gleams in every hand. The angry voices and gory appearances of these naked savages, combined with their excited and frantic gestures and glistening arms, presented an effect so wild and striking that, when I first beheld the scene, I contemplated it in the momentary expectation of beholding one-half of the gathering turn their weapons against the other.'

David Livingstone who spent so much of his life with the natives of central and eastern Africa was also treated to the spectacle of an elephant being cut up and distributed among the villagers. He even ate some meat himself. In an impressive late book on the great explorer's life it is written that, near the village of a chief called Sandia, six of the Makololo shot a cow elephant. The headman of the hunting party superintended the cutting up of the brute and apportioned the pieces,

'the head and right leg belong to him who killed the beast, that is to him who inflicted the first wound; the left leg to him who delivered the second, or first touched the animal after it fell; the meat around the eye to the English, or chief of the travellers; and different parts to the headmen of the different fires, or groups, of which the camp is composed; not forgetting to enjoin the preservation of the fat and bowels for a second distribution.' The cutting up of the carcass was a scene of wild excitement:

'Some jump inside, and roll about there in their eagerness to seize the precious fat, while others run off screaming, with pieces of the bloody meat, throw it on the grass, and run back for more; all kept talking and shouting at the utmost pitch of their voices. Sometimes two or three, regardless of all law, seize the same piece of meat, and have a brief fight of words over it . . . .In an incredibly short time tons of meat are cut up, and placed in separate heaps around.'

The following was the method of cooking the elephant's forefoot, which the white members of the party had for breakfast on the following morning:

'A large hole was dug in the ground in which a fire was made, and when the inside was thoroughly heated, the entire foot was placed in it, and covered over with the hot ashes and soil. Another fire was made above the whole, and kept burning all night . . . . It is a whitish mass, slightly gelatinous, and sweet, like marrow . . . . Elephant's trunks and tongues are also good, and, after long simmering, much resemble the hump of a buffalo, and the tongue of an ox; but all the other meat is tough, and, from its peculiar flavour, only to be eaten by a hungry man.'

Elephants are far less common than they were a million or so years ago and it must be acknowledged that human activity like that described above, has been steadily chipping away at their numbers for a very long time. But the killing has escalated a hundredfold since the coming of the white man. Hunting for sport and the introduction of firearms in the last century or so, followed by the rapid commercial and political exploitation of the continent, have all had their combined effect.

The elephant is very vulnerable to firearms. It cannot hide. Its long reproductive cycle is easily broken. It can be killed easily with a gun and its social way of life can be all too easily disrupted. One well placed bullet can destroy a mother and a calf. Remove a big bull and a generation is lost.

Today the term Great White Hunter is easily misinterpreted. It does *not* apply to the casual visitor who spends a few weeks of his life in the bush trying to bag a specimen or two for display in a foreign country. Neither does it really apply to the hunter in Africa who assists such people in achieving this goal, even though he spends all his days so employed.

It actually applies to a breed of men which has long disappeared from the continent. This was the professional hunter, a tough and dedicated campaigner whose love for the outdoor life could never be reconciled with the enclosed walls of a city – a loner who rarely married. His love for wildlife was tremendous and to put him in his rightful perspective he operated at a time when conservation measures were still decades away. Most importantly, these men did not work for the cash rewards one might have expected them to seek. They operated through an impulse they would have found as impossible to explain as they would have expected any outsider to understand.

In 1929 when the French ceased issuing licenses to shoot unlimited numbers of elephant in French Equatorial Africa, the profession virtually came to an end. The continent had closed in on a rare breed of men which was soon to be replaced by the glory seeker and the fortune hunter of the advancing years of the twentieth century. It is true – and perhaps slightly sad – that there are many people in Africa today with all the qualities possessed of the Great White Hunters of the past.

But they are too late by nearly a hundred years to wander alone in the virgin bush, a lifetime of happy danger from both man and beast, ahead of them.

Even in the 1920s elephants in East Africa were well aware of the implications of gun shots. An elephant that fell dead at the moment of impact from a bullet was less likely to arouse the suspicions of its comrades than one that crashed off through the undergrowth to die several hours later. The hunters knew this and would risk everything to move in close enough for a shot in the brain. The single shot was the last moment in a bush drama that had unfolded over days of careful tracking and maneuvering. Then the hunter could relax, his quarry secure. The tusks were his main prize because their sale would guarantee him the money to continue his chosen way of life. Meat was also cut from the carcass and distributed to locals or dried out and stored for use in the days ahead. It was a hard, solitary existence for a select band of men.

Among the most famous of them was 'Karamoja' Bell who operated in eastern Uganda and western Kenya, the land of the Karamojong tribe. He was fortunate to hunt in country which was still unspoiled and he found large-tusked bulls coming within range at frequent intervals. In 1920 Bell wrote of his astonishment at how he could pick his victim in a crowd and then turn to

Right: With casual pride a white hunter poses for an early photograph beside the elephant he killed at Addo, 40 miles from Port Elizabeth, Cape of Good Hope Province, South Africa.

Above: A white hunter, in the classic garb, poses for posterity beside his elephant kill. After he takes his turn behind the camera.

Above: He photographs his hunting companion, smiling with satisfaction, beside the same dead body.

another nearby without moving. Today – and even then, in most areas – such a luxury would be considered impossible.

Also among this rare group of men was Arthur Neumann. He spent much of his time in northern Kenya near Lake Rudolf (now Lake Turkana). On one occasion he was apparently pinned to the ground by the tusks of an elephant and yet managed to escape death. But there was no recourse possible to the medical trappings of the civilized world. Instead he lay sick for several months while members of the local Samburu tribe administered nourishing milk to heal his injured body. When he was fit enough he was back on the trail of his elephants.

Neumann was one of the first people to notice the habit among elephants of pulling the tusks from the mouths of their long-dead companions and carrying them away to be smashed against a stone or tree trunk. It is a puzzling exercise, centered upon the fascination for the death of a fellow being, and no logical explanation has been put forward for it even today. Perhaps it does not need an explanation in scientific terms; it may be no more than a group acknowledgement of the death of an individual with whom so many close years have been passed. When an elephant has been recently killed its companions will even attempt to cover its body with branches and earth. In humans, such an emotional ritual is called a

burial, and yet it seems to be our prerogative to deny such feelings in other animals.

Neumann became something of a legend in his own lifetime, at least among the natives whose lands he roamed at will. As the network of new administrative policies encompassed his freedom, he retreated more and more to Nairobi where he became increasingly disillusioned. Like many a contemporary hunter, he drifted into obscurity 'like a fish out of water' until he returned to England and died.

There are many other names included in the list of pioneers who operated in Africa around the turn of the century, including Selous, Norton, Buckley, Pretorius, Salmon, and Pearson. One man stands head and shoulders above the rest and, though his history is as yet incomplete he was acknowledged by his contemporaries to be something of a hunters' hunter. His name was Captain James Sutherland and he tracked elephants to their death for more than 30 years, shooting only bulls – unless circumstances dictated otherwise – where others around him would not hesitate to kill females.

In all respects, Sutherland was a remarkable man. His hunting career began in Nyasaland (now Malawi) in 1899, but he soon moved north to German East Africa (now Tanzania) where the nonrestricting elephant license enabled him to hunt full time. His career was interrupted by the

The young Theodore Roosevelt (above left) in 1898 and the writer Ernest Hemingway (above right) in 1950, were among the most celebrated Americans to hunt in Africa in the early years of this century. Hemingway based a book, *The Snows of Kilimanjaro*, on his African experiences.

Maji-Maji rebellion of 1905 and he helped the occupying German forces to crush the rebellion with such effectiveness that he was awarded the Iron Cross.

Sutherland's sympathies did not lie with the Germans when World War I broke out, and he somehow escaped from their clutches and travelled back south to Malawi to join British forces there. He served his country admirably and, by the end of the war, he was back in East Africa – this time as Chief Intelligence Officer – with the Military Cross and the Belgian Croix de Guerre. At this time his love for the bush and its elephants – highlighted perhaps by the trappings of high society in Nairobi – caught up with him. He obtained a special license to hunt in Uganda, the Belgian Congo (now Zaire), and the Sudan. He finally moved to the Upper Ubangi Province of French Equatorial Africa. Among his many exploits, he was once hurled into a tree by an outsized tusker.

Sutherland's passion for his life style was such that he, on several occasions, told another famous hunter, G G Rushby, that he would stay in the bush until the end, and that he wished to die on the tracks of an elephant while he was still active enough to be there. He was, however, very nearly deprived of his wishes by a murderous incident of poisoning. In 1929 Rushby set out from his base camp at Mutobo to track elephants. On his third day in the bush, while he was dismantling a solitary bull he had shot the day before, he was approached by men from his base camp. With them was a runner from Sutherland's camp, bringing the news that the most famous of hunters had been poisoned and now lay close to death in his tent. Rushby immediately packed the barest of essentials and set out with the runner and five of his own men for Sutherland's campsite.

Three days later they arrived to find Sutherland partially paralyzed in the legs and very ill. The poison, made from the buds of a flame tree, had been put into his tea. Fortunately, he had eaten a meal before drinking the tea and, as soon as he felt the paralysis overtaking his legs, he had made himself violently sick. With his meal went the remaining poison and his life was saved. Rushby stayed with him for six days, at the end of which Sutherland's resistance to such an inglorious end had pulled him through. A case was brought against a local subchief, Basibiri, and he and three other Africans were imprisoned for a long time.

Sutherland's spirit was not daunted by the affair and, despite permanent paralysis of his left leg and a health that never fully recovered, he was soon back on the elephant trail. For three more years his exceptional qualities carried him around the desolate bush of what is now northeastern Zaire. His illnesses were frequent but still he refused to return to civilization.

In June 1932, in his sixtieth year, he set out on the tracks of a solitary bull. As he closed in on his quarry he succumbed to the illness that was to be his last. His faithful natives carried him to Yubo on the Sudan border where two doctors were permanently stationed to combat the sleeping sickness that was ravaging the area. Try as they might to save Sutherland's life, the old campaigner died on 26 June.

Even though Sutherland had divorced himself from the trappings of society he was buried at Yubo with full military honors. Some of his friends and a few other hunters clubbed together and collected the money for a headstone to his grave. Its message, inscribed in a bronze plaque set in rough stone, testifies quite simply to the memory of a great elephant hunter.

There was no more than a handful of men who came into Sutherland's category. Between them, despite their modern reputation, they did virtually no damage to elephant populations. If *any* blame for the present plight of elephants is to be laid at their door, it is that they were among the first people to instill in the minds of others – natives who were to become poachers and others who were to become the infamous middle-men in the ivory racket – that elephants could be slaughtered for profit. It is a tenuous thread that attempts to bind together two entirely different worlds. Had those courageous men of a hundred years ago been alive today, their qualities would surely have made them leading lights in the world of conservation.

In the early days of hunting there was much superstition centered around the elephants, and a man who pitted his wits against them was bound to be affected. The natives in the areas where he operated would have filled their lives with powerful omens and taboos and it was a foolish man who ignored these signs and outlawed himself from the very people whose tracking skills and labor he so heavily relied upon. For the hunter whose only aim was to kill an elephant the taboos were nothing but obstructive. What should he care if a particular bird should fly across his path from right to left instead of from left to right, or if a certain reptile should behave the wrong way?

Hunting was considered a man's world and an excursion into the bush was doomed should one of its members have slept with a woman the night before. If the omens were favorable and each man had been celibate and still the elephant proved awkward, then the blame was laid upon the woman who, deprived of her man on the eve of his departure, had undoubtedly been unfaithful during the early days of his absence!

Such superstitions are not confined to Africa. Natives the world over living in close association with animals have woven this respect into their lives. In Borneo, for example, a hunt could be

White gold

The unique qualities of elephant ivory have made it a favorite medium for sculpture since prehistory. It is hard and durable, but easy to carve and relatively flexible; it will withstand changes of temperature, and polishes to a high gloss. Other forms of ivory, such as walrus tusks, may be carved, but never so finely as good elephant ivory.

The first sculptors worked with mammoth and prehistoric elephant ivory. In predynastic Egypt, the working of ivory from elephants in nearby Sudan was brought to a high standard, both in decorative figurines and domestic items such as combs. The craft spread among the Phoenicians and Assyrians, and in classical Greece ivory was a popular medium for statuettes of gods and goddesses. By Roman times ivory was widely used in furnishings and for personal adornments.

As Christianity spread northward through Europe, ivory was used to make ceremonial diptychs and triptychs – the intricately worked covers of ecclesiastical prayer books. Throughout medieval Europe and in Islamic countries, ivory was used to make small – but sometimes lavishly large – boxes and caskets. The carvings on their surfaces are often exquisite, reflecting religious motifs or complex traditional designs.

Ivory carving may be seen at its most intricate in works from China. Ivory was imported from Africa and India along the great trade routes. Some of the most remarkable objects made there include the so-called 'Chinese balls,' in which the delicate carving of the outer surface has holes through which one can admire a second carved ball within, and inside that a third, and so on. They were carved from a single piece of ivory with a finesse rarely equalled.

In Japan the principal use of ivory was for *netsukes* – small figures of people or animals, each bearing two holes in the back which betray their use as 'toggle' fastenings for dress and accessories.

Below: A carved ivory *netsuke* or kimono toggle, representing the Japanese characters Jo and Uba.

Above: An ivory triptych of the thirteenth-century.

These *netsukes* are now popular collectors' items, often fashioned with an eye for a comic scene.

In more recent times the opening up of transport routes throughout the world, and the indiscriminate slaughter of elephants, resulted in larger amounts of ivory reaching the industrial Western world. Ivory was used as inlay for tables, in billiard equipment, and piano keys, as well as for statuettes and jewelry.

In this century, as real ivory has become rarer and consequently more expensive, plastics have taken its place; but true ivory can be recognized by the unique cross-hatched grain pattern that can be seen on its cross-section surfaces.

Above: A Caucasian chair made of solid ivory inlaid with gold and silver, c1810.

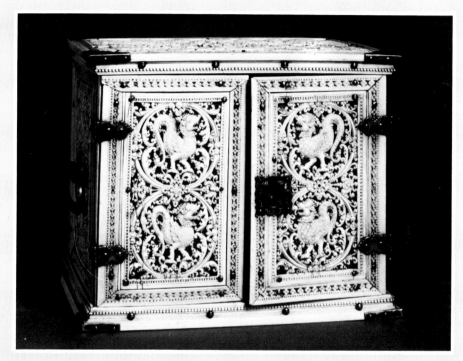

Below: A small, exquisitely carved ivory casket from Sri Lanka, c1700.

Right: Ivory Chinese balls: two or three concentric balls carved from a single piece of ivory.

Above: A small twig, perhaps of acacia thorn, has become lodged in the temporal gland of this elephant (between eye and ear). Such twigs, lodged in the gland and worn smooth with time, are probably the origin of the small pieces of wood which are retrieved by Africans from elephant carcasses and highly prized as magic charms.

delayed for days until the local birds behaved suitably. The point is, of course, that it does not matter how long it takes for the jungle to signal the correct moment to move off in pursuit of the chosen quarry because, until the signs are right, the hunting party is doomed to fail.

All elephants have a gland which opens on the side of the head between the ear and the eye. Occasionally it leaks a powerful-smelling liquid which runs down the side of the face leaving a dark stain. Its function is obscure but it seems to have a strong sexual significance. The Asian elephant is said to be on 'musth' when this happens and it can be particularly aggressive, even attacking its mahout, and is best left alone for the days during which the condition persists.

In Africa the gland is of special importance to natives. A dead elephant will often yield from this spot on its head a small piece of wood which is short and smooth. The elephant probably picked it up when it was forcing its way through thick vegetation but the natives believe it to be that particular elephant's charm, even part of its spirit. For a hunter this small piece of wood was a prized possession and it was carried on every trip into the bush.

Such traditions are now a thing of the past, although a fear and respect for elephants persists among the majority of natives the length and breadth of Africa today. But natives do not hunt

them for food any more. Since the turn of the century things have slowly changed. Elephants *are* killed today but, apart from management schemes, for no motives that can be justified. Something has gone radically wrong. By the 1930s the Great White Hunter was a dying breed. His wilderness was rapidly being overtaken by politics and new laws against the unlimited shooting of elephants. The day of the safari, the organized hunt for profit or trophy, was already underway. Among the pioneers was President Theodore Roosevelt who, in retirement, organized a safari to East Africa in 1909.

The man who lived his life in Africa and became a part of the bush was being replaced by the casual visitor who was detached from his surroundings and interested only in short-term gain. How could the real traditions and values survive as the outside world rushed in for the attractive pickings? Beyond this, the growing human population was taking more land and exerting more pressure on the animals that had roamed free for millions of years. The elephant, with its vast requirements of food and space, was bound to suffer.

The modern trophy hunter – although he has been banned in many a country – is not a patch on his predecessor. He arrives and is escorted into the bush with all the trappings of his civilized world – air conditioning, ice-cold drinks, servants, and inoculation against disease. He might even need to be taught how to use a modern, high-velocity rifle, deadly at a range of several hundred yards and furnished with telescopic sights. Pampered at every turn, he is soon brought face to face with his elephant. His hunter companion will show him where to aim and then stand ready to fire the fatal shot should the first not find its proper mark. By virtue of having fired the first shot the visitor claims the trophy as his own, posing on the great carcass as though it were a life's ambition fulfilled. While the alcoholic celebrations continue far into the night the victim is prepared for its glorious return to civilization.

If the challenge of the hunt is the elephant, the lure is of course its ivory, one of the most valuable materials in the world. It always has been. Ivory was finding its way out of Africa more than a thousand years ago. Even then it was recognized that in both size and quality African ivory was better for carving than Asian ivory. The immediate demands were satisfied by elephants from North Africa but by 700 AD they were all gone and enterprising Arab traders were forced to look to the interior of the continent if they were to continue their highly profitable businesses. Ports sprang up around the coastline and the trade flourished, ranking second only to the export of slaves as Africa's greatest commercial offering to the outside world.

Slaves driven mercilessly from the depths of Africa would carry tusks with them to the east coast. Once loaded onto the waiting dhows both commodities were carried by monsoon winds north to the Red Sea area from where they were distributed, particularly to India and China. Indeed, so desperate were the Chinese for ivory that by the fourteenth century AD, they were coming to Africa themselves to trade directly with the Arab dealers. Slave drivers would often end their journeys to the coast with more than 50,000lb of ivory loaded onto the backs of their unfortunate human victims. More than 500 large elephants would have perished to furnish each miserable column of men that was such a common feature of the savannah lands of East Africa, from the sixteenth to nineteenth centuries.

By the time the interior of Africa was being opened up by adventurous Europeans little over a hundred years ago, untold damage had already been done. When, toward the end of the nineteenth century, the trading in live human cargo was finally stamped out, the elephant was to suffer even more. Chiefs and kings, traders and hunters, dependent upon the slave trade that was suddenly denied to them, turned their avaricious attentions to the wealth of elephants around them with an even greater vengeance than before. The coastal Arabs, once content to sit and wait for the goods to be delivered to them now moved inland distributing thousands of guns and millions of bullets to

Sir Harry Johnston (left), the founder of the British Central African Protectorate, was highly concerned about the preservation of African wildlife. He made careful studies of the animals killed and the damage they did – such as these elephants destroying a palm grove in the Congo, which he painted in 1883.

Jumbo

Above: Despite the exciting novelty of a ride on Jumbo at London Zoo in 1881, the participants have a very solemn air.

Above: Jumbo receives yet another sticky bun thrown by a member of the zoo-going public.

The Victorian age was an exciting time for the amateur zoologist and animal lover. Intrepid explorers and naturalists risked all to penetrate the world's wildernesses, discovering extraordinary beasts and bringing them back – dead or alive. Enterprising entrepreneurs made sure that everyone heard about these amazing creatures.

Although elephants had been seen in England since the sixteenth century, the most famous was the African elephant brought to London from the Jardin des Plantes in Paris in 1865. He was called Jumbo, a name that quickly found its way into popular folklore as a nickname for all elephants. Jumbo was very popular. The general public flocked to feed him buns at London Zoo, and to be photographed (another Victorian novelty) seated on his immense back. He was feted in newspapers, magazines, and even in the music halls.

After some years he became bored by the celebrity life, or perhaps troubled by indigestion from so many buns; at any rate he became bad-tempered and intractable. American circus magnate P T Barnum made an offer of £2000 which the Zoo could not refuse, although the public objected and lamented loudly.

He was warmly welcomed in America, although not the first elephant to be exhibited there – an elephant had been imported from Bengal by Jacob Crowninshield in 1796. He was widely exhibited until 1885. Then, while moving from one circus location to another across a railway line, he came into collision with an unscheduled railway engine. He died an undignified and highly publicized death on the railway embankment. Even this did not remove him from the public eye; his stuffed body is displayed in Tufts University at Boston, and his skeleton in the American Museum of Natural History, New York.

3

Above: Bathtime, luncheon, and dinner: a rather lively account of Jumbo's daily routine, drawn for Victorian children.

Right: The whole family takes a ride on Jumbo's broad back, dismayed at the news that this national monument had just been sold to an American showman.

Right: Jumbo dies on a railway embankment at St Thomas, Ontario, Canada, 15 September 1885. An unscheduled locomotive bore down on Jumbo and the smaller elephant of the circus, Tom Thumb, as they were crossing the line. Their only escape lay along the track, but they were soon run down by the engine. Jumbo died shortly afterward of his injuries, mourned by British and Americans alike.

natives who systematically dispatched the elephants in their neighborhood. By 1870 the southern third of Africa had lost virtually all its elephants and in sub-Saharan regions they were being reduced to well-defined pockets of land. By 1900 it was obvious to anyone who set foot in Africa that the great elephant, plundered for so many centuries, was in grave danger of becoming extinct. But by this time much of the continent was under the control of colonial administrations and new measures could be implemented to put a halt to the wanton slaughter.

Public opinion at home was brought to bear on the governments responsible for foreign policy. The famous Jumbo – London Zoo's African elephant who was sold to America in the 1870 s – awoke the nation to the plight of the elephant in Africa. The length and breadth of England, the word elephant was on everyone's lips as the Zoo authorities struggled to complete the transaction that was causing them so much public embarrassment. Once Jumbo had departed across the Atlantic it was an easy matter for sympathetic politicians to campaign on behalf of the worsening situation in Africa.

Among them were men of the caliber of Sir Harry Johnston who spent many years in Africa 'pacifying' natives and claiming territory for the homeland. Like so many of his kind, Johnston was a fervent naturalist and he made outstanding contributions to science – among them being an involvement in the discovery and naming of the okapi from the Congo forests in 1900. In 1899, at the age of 41, he was sent to Uganda as a special commissioner to reorganize the protectorate following the suppression of a mutiny by imported Sudanese soldiers. Although Johnston retired from African service in 1902, his eyes had been opened to the plight of such animals as the elephant. Johnston's example of dedication and agitation was followed by others and eventually the African elephant became an animal that could be hunted only by the holder of a specially issued permit. Such permits controlled – and they still do – the numbers killed as well as the age of individuals, their tusk size and their location. Of course, it is difficult to implement such laws which look so splendid on ·paper, especially with the worldwide demands for ivory remaining so very great.

The next step was to establish game parks in which all forms of hunting would be totally banned and in which ranger forces would see that the law was upheld. The history of just one of them will serve to demonstrate the good intentions and the problems involved.

On 1 April 1948 the Tsavo National Park was established in Kenya, then a British colony. With the emphasis shifted from killing to conserving, men like Bill Woodley, who had previously appre-

ciated big game only by shooting it, found a new challenge in their lives. Tsavo gave Woodley, still only 19, the chance to stay in the bush and to continue tracking elephants, but now he sought to prevent their deaths at the hands of poachers. His energy and his love of the outdoor life and the animals of Africa were ideal qualities to ensure the success of the National Park experiment. He and his colleagues – Jenkins, Sheldrick, Cowie, Stephens, and others – were up against poachers who sought to supply ivory for money, for billiard balls, for piano keys, and for ornamental carvings in exchange for black market cash that was offered from all over the world. They had 8069 square miles to patrol. In addition they had to combat the easily exploited hunting practices of the natives in the bush. Most natives could never understand why they should go to prison for killing while the white men who had paid their fees remained free to kill again and again. One tribe in particular, the Liangulu, suffered from the enforced legislation and imprisonments that fol-

Above: Mounted elephant tusks flank the entrance of a tourist curio shop in Kenya, where trade in game trophies has since been banned.

lowed elephant hunting. Their tribal mores were shaken by the treatment that they saw as unfairly retaining elephants for the white man alone.

Woodley was concerned and attempted to enroll Liangulus as rangers in the hope that they would understand the sudden change in attitude toward wildlife. It was not a successful ploy and it served only to emphasize the human problems involved in protecting wildlife. Finally, in the 1950s, the idea of game management was seen as a possible solution. There was a vast area of uninhabited land to the east of the Park. The idea was that elephants outside the park boundaries – which existed as no more than lines drawn on a map – would be hunted and killed for their meat rather than for their ivory alone. Some 3000 square miles were set aside for the scheme, which would not only permit the Liangulu to continue their hunting but which was also to bring the tribe revenue for its efforts. The elephants that had been previously cropped by poachers were now to be supervised by the Liangulu.

In December 1958, Ian Parker was brought in to head the operation – the Galana Game Management Scheme – but his initial enthusiasm soon turned to disappointment. The elephants, chased and fired upon from all quarters outside the Park, simply decided to move. They went into the Park, joining those already there, and began to reduce the lush area to a wilderness of damaged trees.

The Park underwent a population explosion. For the first time, scientists realized that concentrations of elephants could seriously modify their habitat, wreaking a destruction upon vegetation that would result in many other forms of wildlife suffering as well. The story of how this particular problem in Tsavo has been faced by the authorities concerned will be explored more fully in the final chapter.

Meanwhile, the ivory trade continues. Figures are alarming, and only rarely do those indicating exports of tusks tally with those imported by foreign countries, particularly in the East. The lure of ivory is like that of gold itself, even though billiard balls and piano keys can now be made from synthetic materials, human greed will ensure that the drain on elephant populations continues. Some say that if gold loses its eminence as the world currency, ivory will take over.

The African continent is itself undergoing a turbulent phase in its political history and the last decade has seen rebellion, and civil and military upheaval in which wildlife policies have been cast to the wind. It has been said, repeatedly, that East Africa has lost more than half of its remaining elephants in the last half a dozen years – the years in which the East African Community has broken down and in which, particularly, Uganda has been without any form of sane government. There is, as yet, no real solution.

Above: Ivory carvers in Zaire, still a stronghold of the illegal ivory trade. Although every last fragment of the tusk is used in such objets d'art, supply cannot keep pace with demand – even though elephants are officially protected.

6:CONSERVING A NATURAL WONDER

Wherever we look in the world today there are animals in danger of extinction. But it is not necessarily a coincidence that they are suffering while man attempts to improve his grip on the world – as natural resources are exploited, as waste products are dumped into the sea and into the air, and as our numbers steadily increase.

Conservationists fight tooth and nail to halt reckless destruction where it can be highlighted as unnecessary, harmful to man himself, or at best identified as a problem to solve. Their successes have been numerous and yet a mood of pessimism prevails. Campaigns are fought on moral grounds, on aesthetic grounds, and on political grounds but the destruction continues. What the conservationists are up against, what they cannot define, is the human nature that is embedded in each and every one of us. We are presently witnessing a climax in evolution as we know it. There have been massive extinctions in the past – can we ever forget the sudden death of the dinosaurs 75 million years ago – and it is easy to acknowledge that they will happen again in the future. But what of the present?

It is today that concerns us, the events that take place while we are alive and struggling as individuals to improve on our own positions in the world. It has to be admitted that for millions of humans the world is not a happy place to live in. How can those scraping to find their food, groping to earn money or those tossed between the political whims of major powers be expected to make significant contributions to the modern wildlife movement which has its origins in the wealthiest regions of the globe?

Should we not, therefore, attempt to solve the human problem before moving on to that of the animals and plants around us, so that we can all work with equal weight, equal conviction, and equal reward? In theory, yes, but we all know that

Above: The map shows the approximate range (in dark tint) of the African forest elephant *Loxodonta africana cyclotis*, in an area that corresponds very closely to the extent of tropical jungle in Africa. The numbers of elephants within the given areas vary considerably.

Above left: The map shows the current distribution (in dark tint) of the African bush elephant, *Loxodonta africana africana*, which once ranged over almost the entire continent.

Opposite: The map shows the current distribution (in dark tint) of the Asian elephant, *Elephas maximus*. This species once ranged west to Turkey and east to China, and included the entire Indian subcontinent. Three or four subspecies of *Elephas maximus* are recognized by some scientists, but the differences between them are too small to be generally accepted.

Left: Is this the future that awaits all elephants? Picked clean by scavengers and bleached by the sun, the bones of an elephant remain, amid skeletal trees in an almost lifeless landscape.

it would be difficult to create a world in which all humans lived with equal rights. Perhaps not all the problems are insurmountable.

So we have to do the best we can for wildlife under the prevailing conditions. These are not good but at least legislation has the advantage of slowing down processes of destruction, giving us more time to gauge the next steps to be taken. With each year that passes these steps become that bit more desperate, because it is not when an animal population reaches zero that it becomes extinct. It happens before then, when numbers fall below a level from which a species can never recover. That is why it is said that in 20 years' time there will be no more gorillas and no more tigers, simply because present and seemingly unalterable trends indicate that their numbers will soon fall below a recovery threshold.

The elephant, already listed as an endangered species in Southeast Asia, is fast becoming one in Africa. Not only is its habitat being fast eroded by man and by itself as a result of man's influence but it is also ruthlessly hunted for its meat and for its ivory. The questions are simple, the answers not so. It is easy to ask how many elephants remain alive, where do they live and what are their requirements for indefinite survival. At enormous financial cost to research programs fairly accurate estimates can be obtained. They will solve nothing if local Governments will not see that survival recommendations are properly implemented. It is not enough to set aside a certain acreage of wilderness – with all the goodwill and tourist money-earning potential in the world – if the population dynamics of the species concerned are not thoroughly understood.

It was not until the mid-1960s that the first serious and scientific study of elephant social life was undertaken in Africa. That was when Iain Douglas-Hamilton, fresh from Oxford University, went off to Lake Manyara in Tanzania and began a four-year project that was to earn him a world-wide acclaim because of its basic contribution to the understanding of elephant livelihood. Admittedly, his findings related specifically to one large group of elephants living in one particular place, but the principles of social organization hold good for elephants covering a much wider area. His findings endorsed many of the tentative suggestions that had been formulated from preliminary studies elsewhere, particularly in Uganda.

The implications of the Manyara project were far-reaching. Above all they endorsed the fact that elephant protection was not enough in its own right and that once the game parks had been created the problems were only just beginning. Not far from Manyara, in Kenya, the Tsavo National Park had already become a cause for concern within 10 years of its being established as a wildlife sanctuary. A decade before Douglas-Hamilton went to Manyara, the warden of Tsavo reported that extensive elephant damage was being sustained by the baobab trees in the Park. For some reason the elephants were stripping them of their stringy bark and plundering their soft, fleshy insides. Great holes were gouged in the trees as the animals went to work systematically.

Within a short time many of the Park's most characteristic trees were lying in shreds. These were the first signs that all was not well with the elephants. The antipoaching schemes, the increased protection of the animals and the failed scheme to compensate the Liangulu tribe had all seemed, in a sense, to be working to the advantage of the elephant. But here they were turning against their paradise and reducing it to a shrub wilderness as a result of stress induced by the artificiality of their new manmade life. A census of elephants was carried out in 1957, producing a figure of just over 2500 individuals in one fifth of the Park. On the assumption that most of the elephants had been counted, the figure was rounded up to 3000 for the whole Park. Only eight years later a full-scale aerial count found in excess of 15,000 elephants in the same area (indicating an original miscount). By 1969 the Park was seen to be holding over 20,000, a figure which should be added to more than 10,000 occupying the thinly human occupied area to the east, between Tsavo and the Kenya coast.

From being an animal in dire need of protection the elephant was suddenly seen to be increasing its numbers dramatically in an area smaller than ever before observed. Although elephants could be seen to be doing extensive damage to the vegetation, reducing a basic woodland community which included acacia trees to open grassland, there were other factors, especially the effects of fire and humans, to be taken into account before any decisions about the elephants could be made.

The pressure to move in and systematically remove a certain percentage of elephants was overwhelming, and seen in many quarters as an obvious solution. It was also seen as no more than a short-term solution, one which would not prevent the elephants from increasing in number again quite soon. Yet, in fact, there was also the intriguing evidence to suggest that somehow the elephants were actually regulating their numbers themselves, to a certain extent – that unknown factors were preventing young females from reaching sexual maturity at a normal age. Perhaps they were suffering from a nutritional upset or their overcrowding was inducing a hormonal response which controlled their reproduction.

It was not only the elephants whose lives were being disrupted by the new way of life. Their extensive browsing altered the ecology of Tsavo to such an extent that fellow browsers – among them the lesser koodoo and the giraffe – were also

The elephant way of death

It has often been observed that wild elephants are very disturbed by the death of one of their number, and that they seem to have an awareness of death rare in the animal kingdom. In *Among the Elephants*, Iain Douglas-Hamilton tells how he saw a cow elephant, recently killed in a fall down a slope, attended by three of her calves: 'The eldest was moaning quietly, but every so often gave vent to a passionate bawl. The second just stood dumbly motionless, its head resting against the mother's body. The smallest calf, less than a year old, made forlorn attempts to suck from her breasts.'

When an elephant is dying of old age the herd usually gathers round it to comfort it, and some may attempt to push it back on its feet. Even after the death some of the herd may stay with the corpse for hours or even days, as if in mourning. One cow elephant was seen to carry the dead body of her calf around on her tusks for several days.

The story of the 'elephant graveyard' is a myth, though a widespread one. The bones of elephants may be found in many places within an area, and indeed given the huge range of some elephant herds, obviously it might be impossible for a dying elephant to reach the 'graveyard' or for its companions to take its remains to such a place.

It is certainly true, however, that elephants have a remarkable fascination with the bones of their comrades, especially the tusks, which may be removed to some distance from the body, or even smashed against trees or rocks. Elephants have also been seen to 'bury' their dead under piles of earth and branches; in a few cases this behavior has been extended to corpses of other species, or even – as reported by George Adamson in *Bwana Game* – to an old tribeswoman who had fallen asleep under a tree.

The causes of elephant death, apart from being killed by humans, include a wide range of diseases – often those that also attack people; accidents, including being crushed by trees weakened by the elephants themselves; starvation; predation, especially of young animals, by lions or tigers in India; and old age – death occurs, from hunger, it seems, when the elephant has lost its final set of teeth and can no longer eat enough.

Left: Death comes in many different guises for the elephant. This young one lies in the parched dust, one of the thousands of elephants that succumbed to recent droughts in East Africa. Left to themselves, the populations of elephants would probably recover from such natural disasters; but now too many manmade factors — such as habitat destruction and extensive poaching — threaten their survival.

In some regions of Africa elephants have caused widespread damage to baobab trees, breaking them down (right) to eat the tender interior fibers. Occasionally the tables of destruction are turned; an elephant (above) was crushed to death by the baobab tree that it had pushed over.

being eaten out of house and home. Similarly, the woodland birds of Tsavo became scarce as tree gave way to scrub and grass. Grazing animals of the buffalo, zebra, and gazelle types found more food available and their numbers increased. The ultimate cause for such a change was obviously human – game parks are artificial by definition – with the elephants seen as the on-the-spot villains of the piece.

In 1969 Richard Laws published a paper called *The Tsavo Research Project*. In it he analyzed all the available data of his own work in both Kenya and Uganda and put forward the proposal that the cropping (systematic killing) of some of Tsavo's elephants might become necessary if the Park was to survive. To many people it seemed a proposal contradictory to the aims of the Park and they were hotly opposed to it. To others it seemed a logical consequence of allowing elephants to breed within defined areas from which they could not move without risk of being shot. The elephants seemed to be intelligent enough to know exactly where they were safest, with the result that not only did they remain within the Park's limits but also that others moved in from outside to join them. As the arguments raged, Tsavo was increasingly battered and bruised by its giant-sized occupants. And no one, really, knew what to do about it.

However, the policy was to become one of non-interference in the hope that the elephants would regulate themselves and establish some sort of natural equilibrium with their surroundings. Perhaps they would die younger or breed later and keep their numbers down to an ecologically acceptable level. What had not been at all predictable was the appearance of drought conditions in Tsavo during 1970–71. Some 6000 elephants perished as a result and an initial examination of the carcasses produced the intriguing fact that they were mostly females and their young that had died – the individuals with whom lay the reproductive responsibility of that year and the future. Had an extensive cropping program taken

Right: Searching desperately for the remnants of water in this rapidly drying pool, a young elephant became trapped in the mud and subsequently died.

place before that dry year descended, the elephants might have faced a serious threat to their survival. As it happened, the drought served to highlight the difficulties involved when man attempts to manipulate an animal of the size and life style of the African elephant.

Thus enlightened people still watch the progress of Tsavo's elephants in an area which has not been reduced to a desert as was predicted some years ago, while the killing inside and outside the Park goes on. There is still time in which to learn how the isolated populations must be treated in the future but the day when these are the only elephants left in the wild, and their survival and therefore careful treatment becomes critical, is drawing closer every minute.

It would, of course, be misleading to look upon Tsavo's elephants as the only ones of importance in Africa. They exist in their thousands in other quarters of the continent and probably nowhere in such prolific numbers as in the vast area drained by the River Nile in southern Sudan. That area, the Sudd, with its endless acres of papyrus swamps is currently an elephant paradise with its natural protection, abundant water supplies, extensive woodland, and virtual inaccessibility to humans. It is also an area in which poachers will tolerate the worst of conditions in pursuit of their financial fortunes and in which, regardless of the wonders of space exploration and men walking on the moon, there is little hope of protective measures being taken.

Once again, despite modern knowledge of elephant behavior and social organization, the largest tuskers will be eliminated leaving chaos in their wake. Kinship groups will be broken up and individuals will wander, like the Liangulu, without identity and time-established bondage. Once this happens the end at worst, or a long road to recovery at best, will follow. The position in Uganda is worth mentioning to show the way in which political upheavals have had apparently disastrous effects upon wildlife.

In just a handful of years during the 1970s – the reign of Idi Amin – Uganda's elephant population declined dramatically. The breakdown of law and order and the absence of any conservation measures over a seven-year period coincided with a sharp increase in the value of ivory. Poachers operated without restraint and carcasses lay side by side over vast areas of bush. Anyone who saw evidence of the slaughter – as I did as early as 1972 – could not help but be appalled by it. Estimates of the year 1976 in the southern sector of Kabalega National Park indicated that elephant numbers may have been reduced from 10,000 to 1000.

However, such reductions have to be placed in a proper perspective before they can be seriously evaluated. The elephant problem is not, after all,

just a postwar problem. At the turn of the century they roamed across some three-quarters of Uganda. Within 30 years, pressures of human expansion and human displacement, following serious outbreaks of sleeping sickness, gave them access to less than one-fifth of the country. In 1925 a department for elephant control was established and it operated on the basic principle that where the interests of man and beast coincided, the beast was to be eliminated. By the mid 1960s, in the Bunyoro District of northwest Uganda, at least 15,000 elephants had been slaughtered under this policy alone. What was perhaps more alarming than this colossal reduction in numbers was that the elephants were being forced to live in far greater concentrations than ever before. They found refuge in new national parks, such as that created around Murchison Falls (now Kabalega Falls National Park) in 1952, where they were forced to stay in overcrowded conditions.

It was in 1949 that the scientific world began to take notice of the damage that was being done, not only to the elephants themselves but also to their environment and other animals and plants. Even so, it was another 15 years before steps could be taken to arrest the destruction. It is never easy to make decisions that enforce the controlled killing of animals, especially when that decision has to be made by people concerned only for the future safety of those animals. Nevertheless, something had to be done in Uganda and despite the unwise slaughter that had already taken place, a program was organized in the mid-1960s to remove under strict control some 2000 elephants. The names of Laws, Parker, and Johnston are those most strongly associated with the program, and it is really a credit to their conviction that such a superficially anticonservation scheme was carried out.

When it was completed in 1967 some pressure on the situation had been released. Further research, however, indicated that at least as many elephants again should be killed in the future if the park areas were to have any chance of recovering their former growth. In 1971 Dr Milton Obote was deposed as leader of Uganda and the infamous days of Idi Amin began. By 1973 tourist trade was at a virtual standstill and there seemed to be a complete breakdown of law and order throughout the country. The price of ivory spiralled across the world and with no official conservation policies implemented, the elephants were at the mercy of the bullet from poacher, soldier, and racketeer alike. Aerial counts over Kabalega Falls in 1974 revealed that elephant numbers had fallen by more than half in a period of 12 months. Within a year the decline had increased to more than three-quarters.

There was no doubt that the elephants had

been killed for their ivory. They lay side by side with their tusks torn from their mouths. Valuable bodies – an elephant weighing 3800lb will yield about 1000lb of meat and 120 square feet of hide – lay parched and neglected. Whereas only a handful of years previously the concern had been that there were too many elephants; now, dramatically, it was that there were too few. It has been suggested, however, that the numbers of today more accurately reflect the space available to the elephants, that the brutal killings have reduced them to an environmentally acceptable level to give them a better chance of survival in the future.

Even if this were true, the elephants have undergone something far more traumatic than a reduction in numbers. Their social organization presumably lies in tatters, a mere shadow of its former self. It can never be too heavily stressed that the elephant is a creature bound closely to other members of its social group. It is dependent upon a way of life that has evolved over millions of years. The breeding success of the elephant depends greatly upon its life style being unimpaired. The opposite has happened in Uganda and huge herds roam the bush seeking only to stay alive. Those who were to make valuable contributions to the next generation may never get the chance. If Uganda's elephants do survive it will be a long time before they regain stability. Today, nobody knows if they will ever fully recover.

In South Africa the elephant is now confined almost exclusively to the Kruger National Park and the Addo Elephant National Park. The former park is partially enclosed but open to immigration from Mozambique in the north. In 1905 there were just 10 elephants in the Park; by 1970 there were more than 7000 of them, an indication of their powers of increase under artificial conditons. The latter park is completely enclosed and a sad reminder of the days when elephants roamed the Cape in freedom. Today they are isolated from the northern populations by almost 2000 miles. They are completely controlled by man, but at least they are there.

In West Africa – the forested home of the smaller subspecies of African elephant – Zaire contains more natural elephant habitat than any other part of Africa. It must be acknowledged that this is largely a result of the foresight of King Albert I who, in 1910, drew up hunting laws to safeguard animals and plants in his kingdom. His predecessor, Leopold II had already established elephant hunting areas as early as 1899. These particular elephants have fared well enough this century, although they were slaughtered mercilessly during the Congo Civil Wars of 20 years ago. Exactly what the position is today is impossible to tell because no estimates on numbers have been issued since independence in 1960. But

Elephants have been criticized for the damage that they do to acacias, stripping young trees of all foliage and older ones of their bark (above) often resulting in the death of the tree. Elephants can destroy areas of acacia woodland faster than nature can regenerate, especially where large numbers of elephants are concentrated in a small area. However, there is a positive aspect: acacia seeds must pass through an animal (usually an elephant) and be expelled in its dung before they can germinate (left).

Elephants may kill as much as 35 percent of the acacias in an area; but giraffes, rhinos, and antelopes also eat these trees.

Above: African elephants in Uganda have been reduced to a tenth of their former numbers within the past few years.

with so much ideal habitat occurring over such a vast area, and despite the fact that ivory that still finds its way out each year, there is good reason to suppose that the forest elephant of West Africa thrives in a way that its savannah counterpart has not enjoyed for several centuries.

In Southeast Asia the elephants are suffering the same sort of problems of reduction in number. As in Africa, their requirements of both food and space are colossal and they come up against similar human requirements wherever they turn. Already they have largely retreated to higher grounds where the impact of agriculture and forest clearance is less in evidence than it is in the lower lying regions. But modern demands have resulted in modern machinery and the human tide is slowly engulfing the undeveloped areas of much of Southeast Asia. Today the Asian elephant occupies a much smaller area of land than that it did a few hundred years ago. Not only this but the elephants live in isolated pockets or 'islands' cut off from each other by another world.

This has led to a phenomenon known as the 'pocketed-herd,' nowhere better illustrated than

Left: A game ranger and the bloody victim of his elephant cull. Such mathematical solutions to the problem of elephant overcrowding are not the best; they fail to take into account the many other factors governing elephant numbers.

Below: The final confrontation: a proud and defiant bull faces his imminent death across the sunbaked bed of a dried-up river. This kill was part of a cull in the name of game management.

Above: A slaughtered elephant provides a feast for vultures and a marabou stork.

on Sri Lanka (formerly Ceylon) off the southern end of India, which is actually an island. The decline of the elephant in this area is worth a closer look, particularly because the elephants now survive in lowland and not highland areas. Before the nineteenth century there were probably in excess of 12,000 elephants on the island. They were captured and exported and also used as war animals – particularly in the 1588 siege of Fort Colombo when 2200 of them were used – and as late as the seventeenth century they were commonly kept in private herds numbering up to 300. By this time the occupying Dutch were also capturing and exporting elephants abroad – a practice that had been going on since at least the sixth century BC.

By the end of the eighteenth century the British had taken over the control of much of the island and they, too, continued to trap and export. Elephants were still present in large numbers and were well distributed. By 1815 local resistance to the British was overcome and the island was opened up for coffee plantations. These ventures operated in the highlands where elephants were still common. With these new commercial enterprises came the huntsman and his rifle, answering the official call to eradicate the pest that destroyed the crops. A bounty scheme paid the princely sum of 10 shillings for each animal killed and it is a little wonder that one man is reported to have shot 1300 himself! By 1891 official eyes were beginning to open to the massacre that masqueraded under the name of control and measures were taken to prevent the wanton destruction of elephants. Some 30 years later it was observed that elephants were becoming a nuisance in areas where they were not being hunted. If this was meant to imply that they were increasing in numbers it was certainly a short-sighted look at the truth. Man was increasing both his numbers and his desires toward the land, and the elephants, decimated in only a century or so, were simply getting in the way. That pressure is still on them. Today it is estimated that there are between 2000 and 4000 elephants living wild in Sri Lanka. They are largely confined to three national parks – Ruhunu (southeast), Wilpattu (northwest), and Gal Oya (east). In theory these parks should be sufficient to contain elephants in such a way that they do not impede human progress. But in Sri Lanka the problems of management and space allocation are accentuated by the locations of Ruhunu and Gal Oya. Both are in areas which sustain annual dry periods and as a result the survival of the elephants is limited by both food and water during several months of the year. The only option open to them is to move toward wetter regions, namely the uplands which are used extensively for coffee and tea plantations.

Below: A herd of some five hundred elephants in Uganda gives some idea of the vast number of elephants that this country boasted until a few years ago. Animals suffered as much as humans under the regime of Idi Amin.

VISITORS ARE WARNED
THAT THE ELEPHANTS
SEEN AROUND THIS
LODGE ARE WILD AND
SHOULD NOT BE
APPROACHED

Left: A passing elephant
at Paraa Lodge, Uganda,
illustrates the message that
his apparently peaceable
demeanor may be deceptive.

These elephant trails were established centuries before humans arrived on the island and until comparatively recently the movement of elephants along them was little more than a slight nuisance to agriculturalists. But the elephant has now fallen into a baited man-made trap. Its migration routes are now lined with succulent foodstuffs, especially sugar cane, and the temptation to feed copiously *en route* to the traditional grounds is too much. Enormous damage is sustained by these artificial feeding grounds, and where the interests of man and elephant overlap, legislation inevitably protects the man.

Thus, despite rigid protection in Sri Lanka, farmers are well within their legal rights to shoot marauding elephants that threaten their financial livelihood. Unless a system of year-long protection for the elephant is devised – and that will entail a certain amount of human sacrifice – the great animal's numbers will continue to slump toward a level from which recovery will be an impossibility. However, such an all-embracing statement tends to imply that people are standing by idly and watching it all happen. This is not true, although the vast majority of people are so preoccupied with their own survival that they do not have the time to spare for other forms of life around them, let alone in a far-off country.

The Asian elephant is more commonly referred to as the Indian elephant. It is popularly thought that India is the stronghold for the elephants of Southeast Asia. But it is their former distribution here and the strength of their association with man that has perpetuated such an idea. Today the Indian subcontinent includes India, Nepal, Bhutan, and Bangladesh. The elephant is concentrated in only small areas in this vast region, mainly in the northeast where between 4000 and 8000 may still exist. On the Indian peninsula itself where they were once widespread they are now found only in the southwest corner, among the hill ranges called the Western Ghats. Some 4000 animals remain isolated there, the highland remains of the populations that were so devastated by the nineteenth-century bounty hunters of the states of Mysore and Madras. The national parks within this area are currently being surveyed by the Southern Indian Task Force of the International Union for the Conservation of Nature (IUCN) – Asian Elephant Group – and it is hoped that it will soon have sufficient information on numbers and movements to be able to implement a worthwhile and lasting policy of conservation.

Beyond India the Asian elephant inhabits a vast area of Southeast Asia. For a variety of reasons, among them politics, culture, and religion, little information is available on numbers and future prospects. But one man – Robert Olivier – has contributed enormously to the Western world's knowledge of the elephant in this remote region. His work in the 1970s was sponsored by the Fauna Preservation Society in London and it must now form the foundation of any conservation-aid programs in the future. Olivier has compiled an

Above: Briefly sedated by a dart, an elephant submits to scientific tests as part of a research program.

impressive document on the past and present status of these isolated elephants and much of his work is here summarized so that the important points begin to emerge from scientific journals and into the realms of public awareness.

China is not a country readily associated with elephants. Marco Polo encountered them in the south, and early Chinese records testify not only to their existence but also to their abundance throughout much of the country. The Chinese, however, did not take their elephants very seriously and they were afforded neither mythological nor religious significance. Instead the elephant became renowned for its nuisance value

to crop farmers and it was ruthlessly persecuted. Nontroublesome individuals were also killed because their tusks and other teeth were an acceptable way of paying taxes to the Imperial Government. There is no evidence beyond this that the animal was used by the early Chinese, and certainly not in any domesticated way.

The elephant problem in China began several thousand years ago when the country expanded south from its former region around the Yellow River and a nation of farmers cleared forests to make way for agriculture. The elephants stayed one step ahead of them, preferring the standing forests to open country. Those that did not move on were killed for the damage they did to crops.

Above: Tourists in Tsavo National Park, Kenya, try to photograph a herd of elephants.

Above: A warden at Aberdare National Park, Kenya, tends an injured baby elephant.

By 1105 BC occasional records of elephants were being documented. One ruler noted how they were driven away from an area – along with the tiger, leopard, and rhinoceros – much to the joy of his people. It was not until almost a thousand years later that the first elephant was used in a captive manner, when, in 121 BC the Emperor Wu received such a gift from the people of southeast China. Elephants were used again occasionally, but serious ventures with captive animals were undertaken only rarely. The strongest evidence concerns the Mongol sovereign Kublai Khan (1214–94) who reportedly kept some 5000 elephants – enough to have built up a colossal war force had the eastern levels of

organization reached those of the war generals of central Asia. By 1900 there were no elephants in captivity in China, a reflection no doubt of dwindling stocks in the wild. By this time much of China's extensive forest had been removed and the elephants, retreating to the south, had moved into countries such as Burma where they have always been revered and domesticated. The Yunnan District of south China is probably the only area to support elephants today. It is still forested in parts and it is one of the few places where the elephant was in the past honored and preserved. Many families kept them and even put them to use in their fields. Northerly populations would have retreated to this area, so even if many were killed there were always new arrivals to maintain their numbers at an acceptable level.

In 1958 the Yunnan Tropical Biological Resources carried out an elephant research program on behalf of the Chinese Academy of Science. Evidence of survival was encountered below 1000m in certain valleys of deciduous trees, bamboo forests, and grasslands. One herd of elephants numbered 52. It was not much, but it at least disproved the theory that the elephant had long been extinct in China.

Olivier puts their present number at about 100. If they can feed undisturbed and raise new young each year there is no reason why they should not increase in numbers in the future. They may now be enjoying a protection they have never known, but there is recent evidence that poachers have caught up with them – the kind of pressure that will drive them into a very early grave.

The Burmese, in stark contrast to the Chinese, have a history of strong association with their elephants. Ancient rulers of the country kept huge numbers of war elephants and in the thirteenth century the king kept at least 2000 in special stables. The practice has persisted well into this century because the elephant has been preserved as a special work force in the huge teak forests. There were an estimated 6000 in captivity in British Burma just before World War II. The figure now stands at around 3500. The wild population in Burma would appear to be safer than in many other countries. The country's forests, covering some 149,000 square miles, are the second largest (after Indonesia) in Asia. Exactly how many elephants are now housed within such an area is difficult to assess and estimates have varied from 5000 to 10,000.

In the 1960s the Elephant Control Scheme was set in operation once more (it was started in 1935 but did not survive the war) and its first aim was a census of wild elephants. In 1962 it came up with the figure of 6500–7000 distributed in the following areas: Northern – 2543; Sittang – 620; Maritime – 1042; Chindwin – 1223; Hlaing – 1017; Shan and Kayah – 343.

The accuracy of these figures must remain in some doubt, especially as the elephant has always been persecuted for its repeated damage to crops. Between 1935 and 1941 over 3000 were killed and at least 1000 captured. This pressure has been on them ever since, despite the favorable estimates of their numbers in the wild.

Officially the elephant remains a protected species and yet successive years of failing legislation, an increase in ivory poaching and a constant drain on wild animals for use in captivity have all led to the official 1977 figure of 5000.

Unfortunately there are no known elephant reserves in Burma, so the wild individuals are highly vulnerable to attack from all quarters. They cannot hope to survive without such protection and it is only to be hoped that some areas of land will be set aside for their safety soon.

There is no up-to-date information on the elephants from Laos. It is centered in a region of the world which has been smitten by war for a great many years and the problems confronting the human population have obviously been of far-reaching importance. Elephants once flourished here – in the 'Land of a Million Elephants' – and yet Olivier was unable to procure any idea of their present status. He guesses that they may still be in the remaining forests, especially in Hodrai Son and the Bolovens Plateau.

Elephants have long been kept in captivity in Laos and as many as 1000 may have been held well into the 1970s. What has happened to them and the wild stocks from which they derived will not be known for some time.

The present situation in Kampuchea makes it impossible to assess elephant welfare in the country. Elephants are certainly held in high esteem and many temples are adorned with carvings and ornaments. There was a time, during the Khmer Empire, when there may have been 200,000 war elephants held in captivity. The 1975 figure was down to less than 1000 used exclusively for domestic purposes. It was also estimated in 1974 that there may have been as many as 10,000 left in the wild.

The last decade, however, has seen a drastic change in policies toward wildlife and the main hope for elephants now is that they are locked away in some of the country's vast tracts of unknown forest. A 1969 report suggested that elephants were still to be seen milling along the Vietnam frontier but that they were also being bombed by American planes intent on depriving the Vietcong of a natural means of transport! Such behavior would have turned the elephants back on their tracks and yet today it is a matter of speculation as to where they are living. There is much potential elephant habitat – most of it unsurveyed – especially in the Cardamom and Elephant Mountains near the coast where the forested habitat remains largely unspoiled. The present political situation in the country does not augur well for the future of its elephants, and even though hunting has been banned since 1958 present attitudes and legislation are unknown.

For many centuries now elephants have enjoyed total protection in Thailand. But theory and practice are not always compatible and it appears that the animals have been under stress of persecution for as many years. At various times elephants have been the property of the king or government, protected by specifically established departments or Protection Acts. But it is one thing to protect animals and yet another to protect the places where they live.

Until the end of last century elephants were found quite close to Bangkok and yet dwindling forests have long since pulled them into the higher mountain reaches. The forests that once covered some 80 percent of Thailand now occupy no more than 30 percent and are being reduced by some 13 percent per annum. This is the equivalent of two million hectares of forest being cleared annually. The reduction in wild stock is reflected in the numbers of domesticated animals. When elephants were numerous in Thailand, as far back as the thirteenth century, they were used to significant effect in warfare to establish the state of Thailand against local enemies. Even in 1884 there were in excess of 20,000 domesticated elephants in the northern regions, each village possessing up to a hundred for its own use. Their demise, however, has been swift and in keeping with the Southeast Asian trend of habitat, poaching, and warfare exercising their combined effect on all forms of wildlife. In 1950 estimates of domesticated elephants stood at about 14,000. By 1969 this number had reduced to 11,000 and by 1972 it was down to 8500. Numbers are still falling and political upheavals, new road systems, and improved technology continue to disrupt the life of the elephant whose numbers now range between 2500 and 4000.

The recent strife that reduced North and South Vietnam to a pitted backwater in the luxurious forests of Southeast Asia has undoubtedly taken its toll in wildlife. Elephants, above all, will have been bombed and suffered many a military indignity as a result of their utility as a means of transport. It is impossible to guess at their present status, although if they have survived in decent numbers their food supplies should be abundant where new stands of bamboo and shrub have replaced the war-devastated forests.

Bazé, in 1955, reports on a herd of 3000 elephants that visited the flood plain of the La Nga River during the wet season. They must have come down from the hills in response to seasonal changes in availability of food and water. Today these animals are conspicuous by their absence and it is a matter of speculation as to whether the forests are now empty or whether the elephants' lives have been disrupted to such an extent that they have gone elsewhere. While it is not possible to give even vague estimates of the number of elephants living in Vietnam, the most up-to-date figure for the area containing Laos, Kampuchea, and Vietnam is 3500–5000.

Mainland Southeast Asia forms the stronghold of a land mass broken up into fragments which have drifted apart over millions of years. Rising sea levels of several hundred thousand years ago also cut off land-bridges leaving a large number of offshore islands. Given the distribution of the Asian elephant during this turbulent period of the earth's history, it is not surprising that it is widely scattered through many of the islands of the region. These populations have varying chances of survival, but all must be considered endangered. In their isolation there is no hope of recruitment from outside if the policies of a particular island are not favorable to their existence.

Although there is plenty of evidence to suggest that elephants are capable swimmers – it is worth recalling the semidomesticated elephant that moved some 200 miles around the Andaman Islands in the Bay of Bengal during the 1930s – there is

Left: Death from unknown causes, probably starvation: but elephants may suffer, even die, from many of the diseases that also attack humans, including diabetes, pneumonia and the common cold. The most common fatal elephant disease is anthrax. There is an extraordinary case on record of an American who died of anthrax contracted from an ivory piano key.

Above: Elephants in Thailand were once very numerous, but may now number as little as 2500.

Above: In an unusual tug-of-war, 60 Thai soldiers prove no match for a single elephant.

Above: Thai royal guards dress in traditional costume for the annual elephant festival at Surin.

Stars of the menagerie

Ever since the days of the Roman Empire elephants have been a popular feature of zoos and animal collections in the West. Henry II of France had an elephant, and Henry IV of France gave one to Queen Elizabeth I of England. In the early nineteenth century the Duke of Devonshire was given an elephant by a lady friend visiting India. The elephant was widely admired for its party tricks, which included opening corked bottles and drinking the contents without spilling a drop.

Another drinking elephant was that in Mr Pidcock's menagerie at Exeter Exchange, which used to have a glass of spirits every evening with its owner. When Mr Pidcock broke the tradition of giving the elephant the first glass, the animal was so insulted that it refused to drink with Mr Pidcock ever again.

One of London Zoo's first elephants was Jack, who was a favorite with the public from 1831 until his death from a throat abcess in 1847. In America P T Barnum, who bought Jumbo (see pages 150–153), had a herd of other elephants; one of them, called Emperor, ran amok in the city of Troy, NY, damaging thousands of dollars' worth of property and injuring several people.

Nowadays elephants such as these in London Zoo are not allowed such close contact with the public as in earlier decades, since overfeeding accounted for several deaths. Their friendly antics with their keepers at bathtime (opposite) and mealtime (right) earn them innumerable fans. They respond well to conditions of captivity although boredom can be a problem. They generally live long and breed quite readily.

obviously no hope that they could resort to such tactics as a means of group survival. However, island situations at least have the advantage of being 'clear-cut.' The elephants live within well-defined geographical areas and their total movements can be monitored more easily than on the mainland where annual migrations might take them from one country to the next, each with a totally different outlook on wildlife.

In theory, it ought to be possible for legislation to give island elephants year-long protection; they need it especially because, biologically, they are isolated and more vulnerable than their mainland counterparts.

There is however evidence to suggest that many of the elephants on these islands were introduced as domesticated animals by man. Many escaped and they now live and breed in the remaining forests in healthy numbers. There is also fossil evidence to suggest that elephants were present at least half a million years ago, during the Pleistocene period, but had long disappeared before the more recent introductions. If man was responsible for these exterminations, then it seems fitting that it is by his hand that the elephants have returned to areas they once occupied unmolested. Nevertheless, the position today is not quite as encouraging as might be hoped.

Borneo's living elephants originated from those

which arrived on the island in 1750, given to the Sultan of Sulu by the East India Company. Some of these animals were subsequently released in North Borneo and it is in this area today that the island's only elephants are to be found.

For a long time, however, scientists have been trying to establish from fossil records that elephants lived on the island many thousands of years ago, perhaps even before the advent of man, and that they were absent, rather than non-existent, until their eighteenth century introduction. The evidence has always been thin and the first record by Von Koenigswald in 1957, a bone from a foot, has since been reidentified as that of an ancient tapir. In 1967 D A Hooijer examined a

partially fossilized molar tooth in the British Museum (Natural History), London. It came from a cave in Brunei, Belact District, North Borneo, and had been in the national collection since May 1910. The tooth undoubtedly belonged to the Asian elephant, *Elephas maximus*, rather than to an earlier elephant-type *Paleoloxodon nomadicus* which was present on the island during the Pleistocene. The Hooijer tooth has also been dated as Pleistocene and, despite the weakness of attaching too great a significance to single specimens, goes a long way toward proving that the modern elephant is currently enjoying what might be considered as a second term of office on Borneo, in the East Indies.

Above: This elephant, displayed in the rotunda of the Natural History Building in the Smithsonian Institution, Washington, DC, is claimed to be the largest elephant ever recorded. It stands over 13 feet high at the shoulder and must have weighed about 12 tons when alive.

Right: A school party of the 1930s looks up in awe at a stuffed African elephant in the British Museum of Natural History in London.

After some 200 years tucked away in the north, the elephants of Borneo appear to be on the move, to the west and to the south, as a result of interference by man. The herds, once made up of more than 100 animals, are now reduced in size. The elephant has officially been protected in Borneo since the 1936 Wild Animals and Birds Preservation Order. Yet the continuous human development of habitat has led to its moving away from once secluded spots and into conflict with agriculture. Crop protection schemes enable it to be shot under such circumstances and nearly 60 were thus killed between 1964 and 1966.

There are no up-to-date estimates of the number of elephants living wild in Borneo. A figure of 2000 in 1949 was confirmed in 1968 and yet this must have fallen significantly since then.

Although there are no elephants surviving on Java island today, there is evidence that they existed there in the past, and quite likely alongside early man. Their remains have been found in a cave occupied by humans some 3000 years ago and they were very likely of the same species that survives today elsewhere. Other fossil remains testify to the presence of elephants on Java in the past but it is not known for certain to which group they belonged. One report from the Pati region of central Java was of a fossil dating back more than 500,000 years to the Pleistocene. It is not known for how long the elephant survived on the island but there is some evidence that the Chinese once imported ivory from Java. The island has long been heavily populated by humans and the disturbance factor would have been enough to remove all its elephants a very long time ago.

This peninsula region was once – and still may be to a certain extent – a haven for naturally occurring elephants. The present-day problems of elephant decline in Malaya are as prevalent as in any other Southeast Asian country but they have been further compounded by a recent lack of cultural appreciation. This has not remedied the paucity of conservation policies, which coincide with forest clearance and expanding human growth. One thousand years ago saw a flourishing ivory trade between Malaya and China. There are even records of prized white elephants being sent across to Yunnan (south China) in the twelfth century. Seventeenth-century Javan imports also originated in Malaya.

These exports by no means reflected the country's attitude toward its elephants. Every Malayan chief kept vast numbers as status symbols and as such their conservation in the wild was assured. A certain amount of trading was acceptable between neighboring countries whose religious and cultural identities strongly overlapped. The favorable attitude toward the elephant persisted well into modern times and in the nineteenth century the animal was still common throughout Malaya. In 1893 elephants were to be found even in the Damansara and Puchong districts which are today buried in the heart of Kuala Lumpur. But by the turn of the twentieth century the elephant's revered place in society was dramatically lost as the modern world engulfed Malaya and the country's unique traditions were disrupted. Perhaps the main reason for this was that the industry of elephant-keeping, as practiced in India where family traditions passed through successive generations, was not present in Malaya. Despite the centuries that elephants had been held in high esteem, they could be discarded for something more profitable, quite literally, overnight.

For some 30 years forests were cleared on a grand scale and rubber trees were planted. The elephant suddenly became a colossal pest. The inevitable result was death on a large scale – with little heed paid to the damage sustained by elephants as long as newfound profits justified any action taken. The 1911 Wild Animals and Birds Protection Act afforded them some theoretical protection against the financial tide that threatened to drown them in the dry land that had been theirs for centuries. In practice, however, it was hopelessly inadequate. The matter was raised again in 1921, in which year elephant hunting by license – with total protection given to females – was introduced.

However by this time the damage had been done. Thousands of elephants had been killed and more were to follow. They had, however, made their mark on the rubber industry. In the Perak's Plus Valley alone, between 1910 and 1930, elephants were responsible for something like £20,000 worth of damage to rubber trees. In a period of 50 years Malaya's elephants, confronted by land development and no serious consideration of their welfare, suffered enormously. They retreated from the west-coast regions and found refuge in the forested hills toward the center and the east, where they were split into isolated groups by the pressures exerted upon them.

The present-day situation is not a healthy one. Elephants still exist in Malaya in reasonable numbers but they are suffering from their past experiences. It seems, however, that they had an official protector in Mohammed Khan bin Momin Khan who became acting Chief Game Warden in 1970. He was a naturalist in a position of power – something completely alien to Malaya until then – and under his control much of the killing was halted. But one man can do no more than slow the process of destruction and Khan was under immense pressure to allow full-scale killing to be resumed. Instead he set up the Elephant Welfare Scheme the responsibility of which was – and still

Elephants in the arena

Elephants have been displayed in circuses in Europe since the Roman Empire. Sometimes they were pitted against each other; sometimes against gladiators, or even unarmed human victims. The Romans also tamed elephants and trained them to dance and perform tricks; presumably killing elephants imported at great expense quickly appeared uneconomic.

The first circus to become famous in modern times was Astley's, founded in London in 1768, and there are accounts that an elephant was one

Above: An illustration of 1894 of a circus elephant; tricks included balancing and stealing apples from the clown's pockets.

of its attractions. In the late nineteenth century, circuses became enormously popular in Europe and the United States. Asian elephants are well suited to circus life, apart from the problems incurred by their size. They often form strong ties of affection with their trainers, for they respond much better to a kindly than to a forceful training. They learn tricks quickly, are surprisingly agile, and usually tolerant of human or other animal co-performers; their longevity makes the effort of training them an excellent investment. It is a pity, however, that the antics which circus elephants are often called upon to perform do not reflect their natural dignity, grace, or intelligence.

Below: Number 1 is shamming death; 2 to 5 perform balancing acts; 6 plays a barrel organ for 7 to dance to; the 8s seesaw while the 9s share dinner; and number 10 walks along a row of bottles.

Today, as wild elephant populations shrink, circuses and zoos are becoming more significant as reminders that elephants are intelligent and charming animals, worthy of every effort of conservation if we are to continue to experience the pleasure of their company. These elephants in the Moscow Circus display their typical ability to learn tricks (and repeat them even after a gap of years; elephant memory is not just a folk legend) and to perform feats of a delicacy extraordinary in beasts of such a size.

is – to trap and move elephants away from areas where they were causing damage. There are no recently available figures for the success of this scheme and it is unlikely that it will succeed in the future. Its existence does, however, emphasize that when people in positions of responsibility feel concern for the wildlife around them it is possible to resort to measures other than wanton slaughter.

The elephant problem in Malaya goes beyond rubber trees. It also encompasses bananas, coconuts, padi, and sugar cane, and the Game Department, if it is to keep its peace with local authorities and members of the public – especially smallholding owners whose interests could be eliminated overnight – is under constant pressure to allow shooting to continue. One hope for the future is that elephants do survive in all the country's wildlife sanctuaries. The most important of these are Taman Nagara, Grik Game Reserve, Krau Game Reserve, and the newly proposed Endau-Rompiu National Park. Whether they will succeed in maintaining healthy populations for an indefinite period remains to be seen, especially as wildlife protection schemes are not fully appreciated in the country and the need for the land is always increasing.

Estimates on how many elephants survive in the wild in Malaya vary enormously. Both Khan and Olivier have undertaken separate surveys recently and their vastly different conclusions indicate the problems involved. In the early 1970s, Khan and Olivier aimed at counting them by recording footprints of different sizes in each of the areas they were known to occupy. They concluded that 556 elephants survived.

A few years later, however, Olivier calculated densities where the elephants lived and then multiplied his figures out across both primary and secondary forests where elephants might easily occur. He was cautious in his estimate and yet concluded that between 3000 and 6000 elephants might still be living in Malaya today. Whatever the true figure, the country's wild elephants have been decimated in only a handful of years, and if present trends of human expansion and unrest continue, Malaya will soon become another country where elephants once flourished and are now nowhere to be seen.

Lying to the south and southwest of the Malayan peninsula is the island of Sumatra. Two or three hundred years ago it was densely populated with elephants which were highly prized and honored members of society. Chiefs kept them in magnificent stables until well into the nineteenth century. Today the elephant has virtually disappeared, the forces of destruction that have been seen across the whole of Southeast Asia finding their way to even this isolated outpost. A 1929 estimate for the island was about 3000 and it compares dramatically with the latest figure of some 300. These animals are scattered in small pockets the length of the island, in such poorly policed reserves as Gunung Leuser and Kluet. Despite their appallingly low numbers, the elephants are still shot and poached for crop-raiding or simply because they are a nuisance. The safest area for them is probably in the north where they remain in the densely forested region of the Langkat reserve. A reserve at Kerumantan in the eastern region of Sumatra is typical of many such areas supposedly set aside for wildlife. Protection laws are not enforced and permits to shoot elephants can easily be obtained from local police. On top of this, forest is still being cleared at an alarming rate. In the south of the island the problems for elephants are essentially the same. The Wai Kambas and Lampung Reserves are the only places where they could now hope to survive if forest clearance was halted. But this seems unlikely and the chances of these elephants becoming extinct are extremely high. Given the dramatic drop in numbers throughout the island and the fragmentation of the once continuous distribution, elephants in Sumatra are seen to be more threatened than anywhere else across the species' range in Asia.

All the indications are that we still have a great deal of work to do in the world today before the future of the elephant can be considered at all secure. At present its numbers are falling rapidly and the overall problem of whether it can survive is compounded by the local conditions where it lives. Pressure from humans is immense and most people are blameless as they fight to protect their own interests. It is the fortune seekers who encourage the illegal poaching of elephants who are responsible for untold damage today.

However there are people who have dedicated and even given their lives to the cause of saving elephants. David Sheldrick is one – a man who before his recent death, toiled with his wife Daphne to find the answer to the Tsavo problem. The battle was against politics, poachers, and the climate, an uphill struggle from the beginning. The dedication to the Sheldricks and their work – a Simon Trevor film called 'Bloody Ivory' – stands as a horrifying reminder to all of us who expect that elephants will simply live for ever.

It is a wheels-within-wheels situation, the smaller representing the greed of humans who have no regard for the state of the natural world around them and the larger representing the simple truth that the elephant is way beyond its evolutionary peak. With our help it could live on indefinitely, and it may be something of an ironical thought that if we show it no concern at all then the forces that could destroy the elephant may one day destroy us as well.

Bibliography

Beard, P H, 1977, Revised ed *The End of The Game*, Rapoport Printing Corp, New York

Carrington, R, 1958, *Elephants*, Chatto and Windus, London

De Beer, G, 1955, *Alps and Elephants, Hannibal's March*, Geoffrey Bles, London

Douglas-Hamilton, Iain and Oria, 1975, *Among the Elephants*, Collins, London

Grzimek, B (ed), 1975, *Grzimek's Animal Life Encyclopaedia*, Van Nostrand Reinhold

Hediger, H, 1969, *Man and Animals in the Zoo*, Routledge and Kegan Paul, London

Jolly, W P, 1976, *Jumbo*, Constable, London

Laws, R M and Parker, I S C, 1968, 'Recent Studies on Elephant Populations in East Africa,' *Symp Zool Soc Lond* no 21 319–59

Laws, R M, 1969, 'The Tsavo Research Project,' *J Reprod Fert*, suppl 6, 459–531

Maglio, V J, 1973, 'Origin and Evolution of the Elephantidae,' *Trans Am Phil Soc* New Series 63 pt 3

Martin-Duncan, P (ed), c 1880, Cassell's *Natural History*, vol 2 Cassell, Petter and Galpin, London

Moss, C, 1976, *Portraits in the Wild*, Hamish Hamilton, London

Murray, N, 1976, *The Love of Elephants*, Octopus, London

Olivier, R, 1978, 'Distribution and Status of the Asian Elephant,' *Oryx*, 14(4) 379–424

Sikes, S, 1971, *The Natural History of the African Elephant*, Weidenfeld and Nicolson, London

Williams, J H, 1950, *Elephant Bill*, Rupert Hart-Davis, England

Williams, S, 1962, *The Footprints of Elephant Bill*, William Kember, London

Acknowledgments

My sincerest thanks go to all those people who have assisted during the researching and writing of this book. In particular I should like to thank all the serious students of elephant life whose published works have enabled me to piece my own fragmentary experiences together.

On the domestic front the book would never have been completed but for the kindness of John Phillipson and Malcolm Coe of the Animal Ecology Research Group, Department of Zoology, Oxford, England. Between them they provided me with working facilities and endless discussion points arising from their own work in Africa and India.

From the same Department I am very grateful to the librarian missisdee (sic) for making her books and her knowledge of them available at all times and to John Fa, Alec Forbes-Watson, Ken Marsland and David Thompson who between them provided various maps, references and useful criticisms. I would also like to thank Jonathan Kingdon whose own work on elephants led me along some intriguing avenues of thought and Humphrey Crick who undertook some vital research before disappearing on his own studies to the depths of Nigeria.

I also wish to acknowledge my great debt to Robert Olivier's article in *Oryx* 1978, which was of invaluable assistance in the writing of Chapter 6.

Quotations were taken from the following sources: pp 18–19, 115–16, 136–40, Cassell's *Natural History*; p 70, *Among the Elephants*, Iain and Oria Douglas-Hamilton; p 140, *The Life and Exploration of Dr Livingstone, the Great Missionary Traveller*, Adams & Co; pp 76–77, 105, 108–09, *Elephant Bill*, J H Williams.

Design: Lawrence Bradbury, Joyce Mason
Picture research and captions: Sally Foy
Artwork: Michael Robinson
Index: Susan de la Plain

Index

Picture Credits

The publisher would like to thank the following organizations and individuals for supplying pictures (a – above, b – below, l – left, r – right):

Heather Angel 72
Ashmolean Museum, Oxford 127, 146–47 (monochromes)
Bodleian Library, Oxford 112b, 113
J Allan Cash 39, 112a, 140, 186
Cooper-Bridgeman 146, 147 (color)
Elisabeth Photo Library 120, 178, 179
Dan Freeman 11, 27, 64–65, 163, 167a, 170–71; 161 (A D Forbes-Watson); 166a (S Harding); 33, 62, 168 (P Lack); 61b (R Lamprey);

159, 174 (K T Marsland); 84 (D Rogers)
Geoslides 107 (top and middle), 111, 148
Robert Harding 107b
Alan Hutchison 53, 79, 110a, 122, 126, 154, 155, 162, 175b, 177
Frank Lane 28, 80, 128, 156–57, 172, 175a, 182b; 66 (J Akester); 85 (A Christiansen); 55 (G Davies); 6–7, 86a (Eichhorn/Zingel); front cover, 31b, 40, 54, 73, 75, 86b (Frants Hartmann); 187 (W Jarchow); 173, 188 (J Karmali); 82b (R Prickett); 45al (M Severn); 57 (R S Virdee); 67 (R J Wheater); 69 (Zimmerman)

Mansell Collection 4/5, 17, 19, 36, 41b, 42–43, 45ar, 45b, 48, 68, 93, 94, 96, 97, 100, 101, 116, 117, 121b, 130, 131, 132a, 133, 138, 139, 149a, 152, 153a, 182a
McQuitty International Collection 47
Ian Murphy 34–35, 38b, 83
Natural Science Photos 24–25 (J Bennett); 115 (M Bolton); 15 (Kinns/Hayward); 31a, 49, 50, 51, 58–59 (Mark Stanley Price)
Peter Newark's Historical Pictures 8–9, 12, 20–21, 102, 121a, 124–25, 134–35, 149b, 151, 153b, 184, 185
N H P A 166b (A Bannister); 30, 104, 105 (D Dickins); 39a, 63 (J Good);

164 (P Johnson); 2–3 (R Perace); 61a, 82a, 103a (E Hanumantha Rao)
New York Public Library Picture Collection 37, 95, 108–09
Oxford Scientific Films back cover, 46, 74; OSF/Animals Animals 71 (F Allan); 41a, 52 (M Austerman); 29 (M Krishnam); 81 (B Smith)
Ann and Bury Peerless 90–91, 98–99, 103b, 106–07, 114, 118, 119, 123
Photoresources 132b
Popperfoto 16, 26, 56, 137, 142, 143, 144, 169
John Reader 87, 88–89
Zoological Society of London 44, 150–51, 180, 181